DESIGNING ENGLISH CURRICULUM FOR ENGINEERING STUDENTS

DESIGNING ENGLISH CURRICULUM FOR ENGINEERING STUDENTS

Kavitha Kondaparthy

INDIA · SINGAPORE · MALAYSIA

ISBN 979-8-89984-419-5

To my late mother

K.HEMALATHA

Who has always been a source of inspiration to me

Preface

With the accelerating dynamic pace of modern technology, English language role in engineering education has never been more important. Engineers need not only to learn technical expertise, but also to present information appropriately in multiform, globalized settings. This dual requirement makes it imperative to revisit and redesign the English curriculum tailored specifically for engineering students.

The Designing English Curriculum for Engineering Students book is a response to the need of bridging the gap between theoretical English language learning and its application in engineering practice. It is based on the belief that language is not a standalone subject but is a crucial tool for professional development, critical thinking, and collaboration internationally.

Analysis and evaluation of curricula form integral parts that are involved in the process of designing materials. A well-planned, proper, effective, methodical, and systematic curriculum has a long way in solving most of the problems that face language teachers and learners. Based on this, the book seeks to evaluate the effectiveness of the English curriculum used by two different engineering institutions. Through this, the book seeks to ascertain the degree to which the existing syllabi satisfy the linguistic, academic, and professional requirements of the learners.

The priorities, concerns, and needs of the students in effect, their real needs, guide the perceived goals and objectives of the English Language Teaching (ELT) curriculum. This research, therefore, maintains the students as the center of the curriculum development with respect to their feedback as being indispensable to the provision of pertinent and outcome-based instruction. The aim of this book is to establish the relative strengths and weaknesses of the curricula prescribed in two different colleges and measure how effective they are in achieving the prescribed and achievable objectives. It also tries to suggest constructive recommendations on how an ideal, student-centered English curriculum that is both suitable to the context and pedagogically sound can be developed.

The chapters address the theoretical underpinnings, models of teaching, testing methods, and principles of material design, thereby offering a complete guidebook for teachers, curriculum developers, and policy-makers in technical education. The arguments are anticipated to enhance the current debates on the reformation of English Language Teaching practice in technical education and stimulate more reflective and responsive curriculum design.

Kavitha Kondaparty

Acknowledgements

First and foremost, I extend my deepest gratitude to Prof. P. Shaila (Retd.), Kakatiya University, for her exceptional guidance, encouragement, and insightful suggestions throughout the course of this project. Her unwavering support has been instrumental in shaping this work. I am also sincerely thankful to Prof. M. Rajeshwar, Prof. S. Latha, Prof. G. Damodar, and Prof. K. Damodar Rao for their academic support, valuable feedback, and constant encouragement. Their scholarly insights enriched my understanding and strengthened the foundation of this book.

I owe heartfelt thanks to my father, K. Rambrahmam, whose enduring values and quiet strength have been a constant source of inspiration. I am profoundly grateful to my better half, Mr. A. Ravinder, for his patience, steadfast support, and encouragement throughout this journey, and to my daughter, Pragnya, for her love, understanding, and gentle forbearance. I extend to them my deepest gratitude for bearing with my busy schedule.

Kavitha Kondaparthy

Contents

Preface . . . . *v*

Acknowledgements . . . . *vii*

1. DEVELOPING CURRICULUM 1
  1.1   Introduction 1
  1.2   Definitions of Curriculum and Syllabus . 1
  1.3   Principles of Curriculum Design 3
  1.4   Objectives of Curriculum 3
  1.5   Conclusion 5

2. APPROACHES TO SYLLABUS DESIGN .6
  2.1   Introduction 6
  2.2   Structural approach 6
      2.2.1   Characteristics 6
      2.2.2   Favourable Characteristics: 7
      2.2.3 Unfavorable Characteristics: 7
  2.3   Situational approach 7
      2.3.1   Characteristics 7
      2.3.2   Favourable Characteristics: 8
      2.3.4   Unfavorable Characteristics: . . . 8
  2.4   Notional / Functional approach 8
      2.4.1   Characteristics: 9
      2.4.2   Favourable Characteristics: 9
      2.4.3   Unfavorable Characteristics: . . . 9
  2.5   Task-Based approach 10
  2.6   Cultural approach 11
  2.7   Skill-based approach 11
  2.8   Content-based approach 11
  2.9   Multi-dimensional approach 12
  2.10 Lexical approach 12
  2.11 Learner-led approach 13
  2.12 Proportional approach 13
  2.13 ESP 13
      2.13.1   General English - ESP 14
      2.13.2   ESP: Definition 15
      2.13.3   Development of ESP Materials 15

  2.14 English for Science and Technology . . . 16
      2.14.1   Needs of the Learners 16
      2.14.2   Diagnosis of the learners'
                 linguistic problems: 16
      2.14.3   Identifying the teaching
                 elements 16
      2.14.4   Syntax of the EST 17
  2.5   Conclusion 17

**3. COMMUNICATIVE LANGUAGE
TEACHING** 18
  3.1   Introduction 19
  3.2   Listening 19
      3.2.1   Strategies of listening
              comprehension 20
      3.2.2   Distractions from listening 21
      3.2.3   Useful listening strategies 21
  3.3   Speaking Skills 22
      3.3.1   The following factors are
              important in the speaking
              process 22
      3.3.2   Functional English 22
      3.3.3   Presentation skills 22
      3.3.4   To make an effective
              presentation one should 23
  3.4 Reading skills 23
      3.4.1   Introduction 23
      3.4.2   Types of Reading 23
      3.4.3   Reading strategies 23
      3.4.4   Schema Theory of Reading . . . 24
      3.4.5   Types of Reading 24
  3.5   Writing Skills 24
      3.5.1   Introduction 24
      3.5.2   Writing guidelines 25
             3.5.2.2 Outline, Revise and Edit. 25
             3.5.2.3 The Beginning 25
             3.5.2.4 Punctuation 25

3.5.2.5 Spelling 25
3.5.2.6 Length of a Sentence.. 25
3.5.2.7 Jargon 26
3.5.3 Modern Writing- E-mails 26
3.6 Computer Assisted Language Learning (CALL) 26
3.6.1 Attributes of CALL.......... 27
3.6.2 The Theoretical Basis 27
3.6.3 Language Laboratory 27
3.6.4 The Role of a Teacher in English Language Communication skills Lab 28
3.6.5 Obstacles of Computer-assisted Language Learning: 28
3.7 Cooperative Language Learning (CLL).. 28
3.8 Task Based Language Teaching (TBLT) ..29
3.8.1 Features of TBLT 31
3.8.2 Tasks that can be conducted on LSRW 32
3.9 Conclusion..................... 32

4. FRAMEWORK OF CURRENT SYLLABI 33
4.1 Introduction 33
4.2 Course Design of I Year B.Tech English, J.NT.U................... 33
4.2.1 To achieve the above objective, JNTU had prescribed the following books:.......... 33
4.2.2 The following is the list of reference books as given by the framers 34
4.2.3 Objectives of the Syllabus 34
4.3 Objectives for LSRW.............. 34
4.3.1 Listening Skills............. 34
4.3.2 Speaking Skills............. 35
4.3.3 Reading Skills.............. 35
4.3.4 Writing Skills 35
4.4 Structure of the detailed text Enjoying Everyday English................. 36
4.4.2 The book is accompanied by an audio CD. The track list has ten units. They are as follows: 37
4.5 Non-detailed text Inspiring Speeches and Lives 37
4.6 English Language Communication Skills Lab........................ 38
4.6.1 Objectives 38
4.6.2 SYLLABUS 38

4.7 III/IV Year B.Tech Advanced English Communication Skills Lab........... 38
4.7.1 Introduction 38
4.7.2 Objectives: 39
4.7.3 Syllabus:................. 39
4.7.4 The following books are to be kept in the laboratory library .. 39
4.7.5 Minimum Requirement for ELCS and AECS Lab: 40
4.8 Introduction 40
4.8.1 Syllabus 40
4.8.2 Suggested Reading 41
4.8.3 Conclusion 41

5. CRITICAL ANALYSIS OF CURRENT SYLLABI 42
5.1 Introduction 42
5.2 Need for Textbook Evaluation........ 44
5.3 Introduction 45
5.4 The Textbooks and the Material....... 45
5.5 Layout, design and price of the text ... 46
5.6 Time Frame for the B.Tech English Programme...................... 46
5.7 Strength and standard of the students .. 46
5.8 Heterogeneity of the class 46
5.9 The detailed text 47
5.9.1 Stating the plan of the text 47
5.9.2 Objectives of the syllabus..... 47
5.9.3 Content and Language Type .. 47
5.9.4 Organisation of the material... 48
5.9.5 Reading Skills.............. 48
5.9.6 Writing Skills 49
5.9.7 Listening skills 50
5.9.8 Speaking Skills............. 50
5.9.9 Grammar 52
5.9.10 Vocabulary 53
5.9.11 Methodology............... 54
5.10 Non-detailed Text................ 54
5.11 Language Laboratory for I -B.Tech.... 55
5.11.1 English Language Communication Skills Lab (ELCS) 55
5.11.2 Advanced English Communication Skills Lab (AECS) for III/IV year B.Tech students................... 55
5.11.3 Methodology 55

5.11.4   Lab Practical Sessions 55

5.11.5   Tasks on writing skills 59

5.12   Assessment. 60

5.12.1   Theory. 60

5.12.2   Laboratory ELCS/AECS 60

5.13   Introduction 61

5.14   The Text books and the Material 61

5.15   Layout, design and price of the text . . . 61

5.16   Timeframe for the programme. 61

5.17   Strength and standard of the students . . 61

5.18   Language Type and Content 61

5.19   The text book 61

5.20   Organization of the material 62

5.21   Comprehension 62

5.21.1   Writing skills 63

5.21.2   Oral Communication 63

5.22   The prescribed Essay 64

5.23   Assessment. 64

5.24   Conclusion 64

6.   FINDINGS AND SUGGESTIONS 65

6.1   Introduction 65

6.2   Role of the teacher (traditional teacher
vs. modern teacher) 65

6.3   Role of the student 66

6.4   Heterogeneity of the class 66

6.4.1   Language levels and general
traits of learners 67

6.4.2   Self-Assessment by the Student: 68

6.5   Methodology 69

6.5.1   Computer Assisted Language
Learning 70

6.6   Syllabus Revision 70

6.7   Timeframe 70

6.8   Lack of facilities 71

6.9   Untrained teachers/Lack of technical
knowledge in language teacher 71

6.10   Inappropriate assessment 71

6.11   Evaluation and Feedback 72

6.12   JNTU Syllabus: Findings and
suggestions. 72

6.12.1   The text and other material. . . . 72

6.12.2   Relevance of course content . . . 72

6.13   Vocabulary 73

6.13.1   Fill in the blanks choosing the
word from the list and complete
the following sentences.
(Technical extract from net) . . . 73

6.13.2   Write a short story using the
words from the list with the help
of following hints. 73

6.13.3   Form the words with the given
prefix and suffixes and use the
words in own sentences. One is
done as an example. 74

6.13.4.   Choose the right pair of words
which has the similar correlation
as the question analogy pair of
words has. 74

6.13.5   Look at the word list and put a
tick mark against the familiar
words and write the meanings.
Then use the words in own
sentences. This can be done
individually or pair or group. . . 74

6.13.6   Tick the right word for
the following exercises
on synonyms, antonyms,
homonyms, homophones and
homographs. The exercises can
be developed as follows: 74

6.13.7   Select a topic on which list out
as many related words as you
can and share with friends.
(Topics can be given by the
teacher or can be chosen by the
student). 74

6.13.8   Pick the words from the list
given below, write other forms
(different parts of speech) of
those words and use them in
different sentences. 74

6.13.9   Crossword games 75

6.13.10 Write short dialogues as pair
work using idioms/phrasal
verbs/one word substitutes
choosing from the list. 75

6.14   Teaching macro Skills through text 75

6.14.1   Reading comprehension 76

6.14.2   Recommended Reading and
software 77

6.15 Introduction 78

6.16 The textbook and other material 78

6.17 The syllabus is not able to fulfill its
      objective because 78

6.18 The objectives of the course must be
      student centric 78

6.19 Suggestions 79

6.20 Concluding Remarks 79

7.   **CONCLUSION** 80

      7.1. Suggestions at a glance: 81

Select Bibliography 84

CHAPTER 1

Developing Curriculum

Chapter I presents introduction to the issues of curriculum design. It provides the definitions of curriculum, reviews various aspects of curriculum formulation like principles, objectives, and approaches. It provides a background against which the whole study is made placing it in the perspective of English Language Teaching and Course Design.

1.1 INTRODUCTION

The aim of the curriculum is to fulfill the needs of the learner. In recent years there has been an increasing agreement among syllabus planners, teachers and learners that English Language courses should incorporate learner's future language needs into the course design. Researches on ELT claim that there is a need for improvement in designing curriculum to suit the changes in the world situation. Therefore, the necessity to make the curriculum appropriate for the present situation has been felt. Inventories were sequenced, integrated and then presented to the methodologists and it was their task to build up learning activities to facilitate the learning of the pre-specified content. In this context a theoretical background of curriculum design and issues related need to be studied.

1.2 DEFINITIONS OF CURRICULUM AND SYLLABUS

The terms "curriculum" and "syllabus" are similar in meaning but they discern each other. Traditionally syllabus has been regarded as the content of a course, or the subject matter to be covered whereas curriculum is a statement of what the course is trying to do, as stated in the objectives. According to Nunan,

Curriculum is planning, decision making, in relation to learners' needs and purposes; establishing goals and objectives; selecting and grading contents; organizing appropriate learning arrangements; selecting, adapting, and developing appropriate leaning materials, learning tasks, assessment and evaluation. The syllabus represents narrowly on the selection and gradation of contents. (13)

Dubin and Olshtain, describe a syllabus as a "… detailed and operational statement of teaching and learning elements which translates the philosophy of the curriculum into a series of planned steps leading towards more narrowly defined objectives at each level" (28). According to White:

…syllabus refers to the content or subject matter of an individual subject, whereas curriculum refers to the totality of content to be taught and aims to be realized within one school or educational programme. (77)

Graves states that "Curriculum will be understood in the broadest sense as the philosophy, purpose, design and implementation of a whole programme. Syllabus will be narrowly defined as the specification and ordering of content of a course or courses" (3). Stenhouse says, "Curriculum is a basis for planning a course, studying it empirically and considering the grounds of its justification" (5).

Breen declares: "A syllabus expresses, however indirectly, certain assumptions about language, about the psychological process of learning and about the pedagogic and social processes within a classroom" (52). Richards C. Platt and Platt define "Curriculum as an educational programme which states: a) the educational purposes of the programme (the ends) b) the content, teaching procedures and learning experiences which will be necessary to achieve this purpose (the means) c) some means for assessing whether or not the educational ends have been achieved" (94).

Ralph Tyler expressed analogous views on curriculum in his book *Basic Principles of Curriculum and Instructions* which is divided into five sections. Each of the first four sections is titled with a question as:

1. What educational purpose does the school seek to attain?
2. What educational experiences can be provided that are likely to attain these purposes?
3. How can these educational purposes be effectively organized?
4. How can we determine whether these purposes are being attained?

M. L. Tickoo in his "English for Specific Purposes: A Learner-centered Approach," says that curriculum must reflect,

1. current thinking on what language is,
2. how best it is acquired,
3. a similar awareness of new thinking on classroom management,
4. ways of building a conducive learning environment (92-99).

Prabhu says that "The syllabus is a form of support to the teaching activity that is to be carried out in the classroom and a form of guidance in the construction of appropriate lesson plans" (86). Thus the syllabus is an "operational construct", and is concerned with procedures of teaching. According to him, the syllabus is also an "illuminative construct" concerned with the product of learning, as it is a specification of what is to be learnt in terms of a conceptual model which provides an understanding of the nature of the subject area concerned.

Brumfit (1979) asserts that a syllabus is an implicit statement of views on the nature of language, language learning and language use. Stern (1984) defines syllabus as connected with content, structure and organization, while curriculum development is viewed as connected with implementation, dissemination and evaluation. Eisner and Vallace assert the curriculum can be acknowledged as a statement which is concerned with "what can and should be taught to whom, when and how" (2).

Hutchinson and Waters describe syllabus as, "… at its simplest level a syllabus can be described as a statement of what is to be learnt. It reflects of language and linguistic performance" (80). Yalden takes syllabus as a "… summary of the content to which learners will be exposed" (87). According to Lee, "Syllabus is essentially a statement of what should be taught year by year, though language syllabuses often also contain points about the method of teaching and the time to be taken"(108).

The varied definitions create perplexity, however to sum up in Brown's words, "Curriculum is a wide description of general goals by indicating the whole educational-cultural philosophy which applies across subjects together with a theoretical orientation to language and language learning while syllabus design can be defined as selection and organization of instructional content including suggested strategy for presenting content and evaluation."

1.3 PRINCIPLES OF CURRICULUM DESIGN

According to Stenhouse, principle of curriculum is "...an attempt to communicate the essential features and principles of an educational proposal in such a form that it is open to critical scrutiny and capable of effective translation into practice. It should provide a basis for planning a course, studying it empirically and consider the grounds of its justification." He thought that it should aim at the following:

- Selection of content - what is to be learnt and taught.
- The development of a teaching strategy - how it is to be learned and taught.
- Making of decisions about sequence.
- Principles on which to diagnose the strengths and weaknesses of individual students.
- To study and evaluate the progress of students.
- To study and evaluate the progress of teachers.
- A formulation of the intention or aim of the curriculum which is accessible to critical scrutiny. (5)

Hutchinson and Waters state that "Course design answers certain fundamental questions in order to provide a rationale for the subsequent processes of syllabus design materials writing, classroom teaching and evaluation".

The fundamental questions according to them are:
1. Why does the student need to learn?
2. What does the student need to learn?
3. What aspects of language are needed and how will they be described?
4. How will the language learning be achieved? (59)

These questions are based on the needs of the students in learning the target language, the objectives, the content of the language, the linguistic aspects, the theories of language learning, and the teaching methodology.

Candlin states the fact that while curriculum is connected with "language learning, learning purpose and experience, evaluation, and the role relationships of teachers and learners" (30), syllabus is a more concrete term, referring to the actual events in the classroom, i.e. the application of a syllabus to a given situation.

Nunan's idea on syllabus design is that "it should consist of the elements like: a) Needs Analysis b) Goals and Objectives c) Content specification d) Learning tasks and activities e) Resources and material f) Learner assessment or evaluation" (213). He argues that the curriculum is the totality of what actually happens in an educational setting.

Jack C. Richards has similar views about syllabus design in "Language Curriculum Development." They are:
- Determining the needs of a particular group of learners
- Developing objectives for a language course to meet the said needs
- Selecting teaching and learning activities and experiences that will enable these needs to be realized
- Evaluating the outcomes (25-32).

1.4 OBJECTIVES OF CURRICULUM

The needs of the learners determine the contents of the curriculum. The analysts collect information about learner's needs, social expectations, learning constraints and the resources available for implementing the programme. The needs of the learners depend upon the stage of their learning. Based on the needs of the learners, objectives of the syllabus will be formulated. The objectives of a course direct the selection of the course content, structure, functions, notions, methods and tasks. Clear understanding of the curriculum objectives help the teachers to be certain what material to teach, and at what time and how it should be taught. In his book *The Learner-centered Curriculum*, D. Nunan gives a clear description of how one should state objectives. Based on what is desired, objectives may sound like the following:

- Students will learn …
- Students will be aware of …
- Students will develop …

He observes that objectives give a clear perception to teachers and the learners get the awareness of what they can expect from a language programme. He classifies objectives into two types: i) process objectives ii) product objectives. Process oriented objectives focus on the activities but not on the outcomes of the instruction, whereas product oriented objectives describe the things that a learner will be able to do as a result of instruction.

According to Hutchinson, Waters and Richards, "Objectives define the content of a syllabus. The content of a syllabus is specific in terms of language aspects such as vocabulary, functions, notions, grammar or specific listening, speaking, reading or composing skills and the topics related to the needs of the learner are included" (80).

Graves explains that "… formulating goals and objectives for a particular course allows the teacher to create a clear picture of what the course is going to be about and goals are general statements or the final destination of the level the students need to achieve" (3). Objectives express certain ways of achieving the goals. In other words, objectives are teachable chunks, which in their accumulation form the essence of the course. Clear understanding of goals and objectives will help teachers to be sure what material to teach, and when and how it should be taught.

Widdowson prospected on objectives of curriculum as,

- To develop the skills necessary to take part in academic study.
- To obtain sufficient oral and written skills.
- To communicate socially in the target language.
- To develop the survival skills.
- To be able to read the literature of the target culture. (201-212)

As is evident from above, the term 'curriculum' and 'syllabus' are used synonymously by many. For the present purpose curriculum is used in the sense of a comprehensive plan on which the system of learning and teaching are based. The syllabus represents the picture, a particular stage of this overall plan. The courses are the tools used to achieve the objectives piecemeal as one moves from one stage to another. The framers of the curriculum in this context have the responsibility to define completely the educational needs of the learner and identify the means through which these need to be fulfilled. Curriculum development according to Nunan at least has three phases:

- Planning phase
- Implementation phase
- Evaluation phase

The syllabus for Widdowson is simply a framework within which activities can be carried out. It is a teaching device used to facilitate teaching in the class.

Curriculum planning addresses the needs of the learners and resources requisite for carrying out intended actions. It involves establishing and determining how to administer policy that will govern the planned actions.

Nunan says, "During the 1970s, needs analysis procedures made their appearance in language planning" (43). Methods and procedures for gathering information to be used in syllabus design are referred to as 'needs analysis', which comprises specification of objectives through interviews, questionnaires, observations. The curriculum designers consider the particulars of learner's age, nationality, mother tongue, current proficiency level, perceptions, goals and priorities. The curriculum implementation phase covers syllabus of a programme, content of the teaching material, methods of teaching and time frame for the programme. The teacher follows the policy of the curriculum and involves actively in the process of implementation. The last and crucial phase of the curriculum process is evaluation which assesses the achievement of the student's course objectives by conducting tests and gathering feedback from the students about course relevance.

1.5 CONCLUSION

Education is most often seen as a scientific exercise in which objectives are set, a plan drawn up, applied and the outcomes measured. Therefore curriculum is like a blueprint which offers an entire plan for a teaching programme. The designers of a curriculum follow various approaches.

It is essential for the designers to make a decision as to what is to be taught and in what order while designing the syllabus. The choice of an approach and the designing of a syllabus is the most important step in making the teaching, learning process an accomplishment. A great deal of confusion persists as to what type of content should go into a syllabus and the methodology to be adopted in teaching. Quite a few distinct types of language teaching syllabi exist which may be implemented in various teaching situations according to the needs of the learners. The next chapter discusses various approaches used in the process of syllabus design.

CHAPTER 2

Approaches to Syllabus Design

2.1 INTRODUCTION

The teaching of English in India is centered on teaching materials. A Syllabus designer's views on the nature of learning, the type of teaching to be adopted and the content to be incorporated play a crucial role in designing the syllabus for any stream of learners. Syllabus design is the basic component of curriculum development. Various types of approaches based on various language assumptions abound on the material production scene. The fundamental task before today's course designer is to understand the needs of the learners and basing on it select an approach, specify it, design the material and grade the learning tasks and activities accordingly.

2.2 STRUCTURAL APPROACH

Structural Syllabus is the most prevalent and is known by various other names like Grammatical Syllabus, Formal Syllabus, Traditional Syllabus and Synthetic Syllabus in which grammatical structures form the central organizing principle. This approach obtains its content mainly from the structural linguists. The learner is expected to master each structural step and the focus is on the outcome or the product. It is evident in this syllabus that the focus is on the knowledge and skills which learners should acquire as a consequence of instruction, not on how they can attain them. According to Wilkins:

> A synthetic language teaching strategy is one in which the different parts of a language are taught separately and step by step so that acquisition is a process of gradual accumulation of the parts until the whole structure of the language has been built up. (14)

The content of the structural syllabus rests on two components. 1. The Linguistic composition (grammar the forms and structures, usually nouns, verbs, adjectives, statements, questions, subordinate clauses, and so on.) 2. A list of words (lexicon). Its objective is to make the learner master the grammar rules of the target language. In addition, it is also expected that the students will learn adequate basic vocabulary.

2.2.1 Characteristics

The following are the characteristics of this approach:

1. It comprises of a set of grammatical rules. After learning the rules one relates them to practical language use.
2. The syllabus component is selected and graded based on grammatical notions of

simplicity and complexity. These syllabi initiate one item at a time and require mastery of that item before moving on to the next.

3. This syllabus maintains that it is easier for students to acquire language if they are exposed to one element of the grammatical system at a time.

Basically the linguistic components and their performance are analyzed. Subsequently the language is broken down into small grammatical components and presented in a strictly controlled sequence. The sequence is set in accordance with increasing intricacy, from simple grammatical structure to more complex grammatical structure. To teach this syllabus Audio-lingual Method or Grammar Translation method are followed.

2.2.2 Favourable Characteristics:

This syllabus is favourable on the following grounds:

1. The learner moves from simple to complex grammatical structures and may understand the grammatical system more easily.
2. It is very much helpful in building up writing skills.
3. It enriches student's basic vocabulary.

2.2.3 Unfavorable Characteristics:

It is not favorable on the following grounds:

1. It exaggerates language structure and ignores communicative competence.
2. It does not deal with the instantaneous communication needs of the learner.
3. The student's role is passive, since it is the teacher who decides what to teach in which state.

A fundamental criticism is that the grammatical syllabus focuses on only one element of language, namely grammar, whereas in truth there exist many more aspects to language.

2.3 SITUATIONAL APPROACH

The drawbacks and limitations of structural syllabus led to a substitute approach where situational needs are focused rather than grammatical units. The main purpose of a situational language teaching syllabus is to teach the language which occurs in the situations. According to Wilkins, "Motivation will be heightened since it is learner, rather than subject centered" (14).

A collection of real or imaginary situations form the content of language teaching. A situation generally involves several participants who are engaged in some activity in a specific setting. The language which occurs in the situation involves a number of functions, combined into a plausible segment of discourse. Examples of situations include: at the bank, at the supermarket, at a restaurant, seeing the doctor, complaining to the landlord, purchasing stationary at a book stall and so on. Whatever be the methodology adopted in teaching, the teacher's role is that of a facilitator.

2.3.1 Characteristics

1. The principal organizing characteristic and the focus is on the situations which reflect the way language and behaviour are used every day outside the classroom.
2. By relating structural theory to situations the learner becomes proficient to deduce the meaning from the relevant context.
3. It emphasizes methodology and learning processes.

It is associated with the development of understanding, not just the inert reception of knowledge or the acquisition of specific skill.

2.3.2 Favourable Characteristics:

This syllabus is favourable on the following grounds:

1. A practical command over the basic language skills through structure.
2. Accurateness in both pronunciation and grammar.
3. It is learner-centered rather than subject centered.

2.3.4 Unfavorable Characteristics:

It is not favorable on the following grounds:

1. It is difficult to implement the syllabus since the situation itself is difficult to define.
2. This syllabus will be limited for students whose real needs are not fulfilled by the situations.
3. This syllabus may not predict and incorporate the language necessary to handle the language situation. The cultural difference may be a factor influencing the learner.

The defect of this syllabus is that it is difficult to implement since the situation itself is difficult to define. Though the exact contents of the situational syllabus are the consequence of a careful behavioral prediction, consisting of an inventory of language situations and an account of the linguistic content of these situations, the situational syllabus will not be able to incorporate all the situations in real life.

Subsequently, the situational syllabus may not predict and include the language necessary to handle the language situation. The language necessary to perform linguistically in situations is taught, though the language used for the same situations may be unpredictable. Learners give diverse responses to the same situations because of their previous life experiences, intentions, as well as their views of the world. The limited aims of a tourist, a waiter or a telephone switchboard operator might be achieved adequately under the controlled situations. However, they would be unprepared for anything 'out of the ordinary' (Rabbini). Wilkins argues that situational syllabus only includes language functions that occur in specific situations (14).

Brumfit and Johnson also address the problems with the situational syllabus such as the limited horizons of language in specific situations and difficulty in defining what the situation is in the first place (84). It's true that language is closely related to situations. In some situations certain intentions are regularly expressed, certain linguistic transactions regularly carried out, but this does not mean that they are typical of the language use. Moreover, the making of complaints and requests, the seeking of information, the expression of agreement and disagreement can take place in almost any situation. There are probably no situations where one typically expresses possibility, probability, certainty, doubt or conviction. The situational syllabus seems to provide with examples of general language use in specific situations. A situational syllabus is limited, and learners real needs are not covered by the situations in the syllabus. This led Wilkins to describe notional and communicative categories that had a significant impact on syllabus design.

2.4 NOTIONAL / FUNCTIONAL APPROACH

Notional-functional approach pays no attention to grammatical structure but rather pays attention to "notions and functions" of language. The notion is the context and the function is the purpose of speaking. The content of the language teaching is a compilation of the functions that are executed when language is used, or of the ideas that language is used to express. These functions include: giving information, agreeing with others, apologizing, requesting etc., Examples for notions include size, age, color, comparison, time and so on.

It is primary and inevitable to establish objectives. For this the needs of the learners have to be examined for the various types of communication that they require to do. As a result, needs analysis has connection with notional-functional syllabi. Though needs analysis implies a focus on the learner in this approach, critics suggest that a new list has replaced the old one. Where once structural/situational items were used, now a new list consisting of ideas and functions has become the main focus in a syllabus. White claims that "language functions do not usually occur in isolation and there are also difficulties of selecting and grading function and form" (77).

Learners' communicative needs come first in functional-notional approach. What the learner wishes to communicate is taken as its starting point. This may be done intuitively based on experience, and/or by means of questionnaires or interviews. Language teaching is then planned in terms of content rather than form. In its original form, a language program founded on functional-notional principles consists of sequenced sets of oral and written functions, beginning with those most required for survival and finishing at a proficiency level adequate for the learner to communicate successfully, but not natively nor near-natively. According to Barnett "importance is given to (a) sentences in combination instead of the sentence as the basic unit in language teaching (b) meaning (or communication) over form which reduces the attention given to grammar and the importance assigned to grammatical accuracy (c) participation in authentic language use (d) fluency and appropriateness in learner performance over formal accuracy, (e) speaking and listening skills in class" (44).

2.4.1 Characteristics:

Barnett proposes the characteristics as follows:

1. A functional view of language focusing on doing something through language
2. A semantic base, as opposed to a grammatical or a situational base.
3. A learner-centered view of language learning (Barnett 43).

2.4.2 Favourable Characteristics:

This syllabus is favorable on the following grounds:

1. The learners learn to use language for their communicative purposes.
2. The syllabus is flexible and admission of students into the syllabus is feasible at any point of time.
3. The syllabus promotes language variation since learners may choose from a diverse range of expressions and grammatical patterns to perform each communicative function.

2.4.3 Unfavorable Characteristics:

It is not favorable on the following grounds:

The functional-notional syllabus looked a very sensible idea at the time; however, there are problems in defining and specifying such a syllabus.

1. The vast complexity of the task of developing the content of language syllabuses in this way remains a major problem.
2. The major problem with such lists is the intricacy of defining functions with precision and clarity. The absence of set conditions (or contextual factors) which limit or determine analysis of a given function means that there is at best some ambiguity, and at worst an entire misunderstanding over what is meant by such functions for instance, expressing opinion or expressing dissatisfaction may

mean the same i.e., as one not obliged to do something.

3. A single language function "inviting" may be expressed in many ways by using various exponents in different contexts e.g., formal vs. informal contexts. Sometimes this causes confusion and frustration in learners resulting in their failure to determine which exponent to use in a given situation.

4. It is argued that the limited findings of functions in functional-notional syllabi are not different from inventories of language rules. For example, instead of learning "the simple past tense," learners might be required to talk about the things that the learners did last week. Therefore, the problems are basically the same; being able to perform specific functions does not equal language competence as a whole.

2.5 TASK-BASED APPROACH

The deficiencies in the product oriented syllabi caused for process oriented syllabi. In this syllabus the focus is not on what the learner will have accomplished on completion of the course, but on the specification of learning tasks and activities that the learner will undertake during the course.

A task-based syllabus focuses on learning processes or learner rather than linguistics. It emphasized utilizing tasks and activities to encourage learners to use the language communicatively so as to achieve a purpose. It signifies that speaking a language is a skill best perfected through interaction and practice. The most significant point is that tasks must be relevant to the real language needs of the learner. It should be a meaningful task so as to improve learning. The content of the teaching is a series of comprehensive and focused tasks that

the students need to perform with the aid of the language they are learning. These tasks combine language and other skills in particular contexts of language use. The best classic example of this syllabus is Prabhu's *Bangalore Project*.

The tasks are described as activities with a purpose other than language learning. But as in a content-based syllabus, the presentation of the tasks is organized in a way that proposes to develop second language ability. Language learning is secondary to task performance, and language teaching takes place only as the need arises during the performance of a given task. Tasks incorporate language (and other) skills in specific settings of language use. Task-based teaching differs from situation-based teaching in that while situational teaching has the goal of teaching the specific language content that occurs in the situation (a predefined product), task-based teaching has the goal of teaching students to draw on resources to complete some piece of work (a process). The students draw on their choice of language forms, functions and skills, often in an individual and unexpected way, in completing the tasks. Tasks which can be used for learning language are generally, tasks that the students actually have to perform in any case. For example applying for a job, talking with a shop keeper, getting information for accommodation over the telephone etc. can be considered as tasks.

By taking part in the tasks such as information giving and opinion-gap activities, it was hoped that the learner would acquire the language subconsciously while consciously focusing on solving the meaning behind the tasks.

A task-based approach presumes that using the language is a skill best performed through practice and INTERACTION. It uses activities to give confidence to learners to use the language communicatively in order to achieve a purpose. Tasks must be applicable to the real language needs of the student. The fundamental learning theory of the task based and communicative language teaching appears to suggest that activities which employ language to complete meaningful tasks enhance learning. This type of syllabus was supported by Breen who says that:

> A framework can be offered within which either a pre-designed content syllabus can be openly analyzed and evaluated by the classroom group, or a developing content syllabus can be designed in an on-going way.(52)

It offers a frame for decisions and substitute procedures, activities and tasks for the learners. It explicitly attends to teaching and learning and takes into consideration the possible interrelationships between subject matter, learning and the latent contribution of a classroom.

2.6 CULTURAL APPROACH

Stern argues for "cultural syllabus" to be incorporated into second/foreign language education. Defining the concept of 'culture' is a challenging task. Seelye refused to define culture, calling it "a broad concept that embraces all aspects of the life of man" (26) and Brown calls it the "glue" that binds a group of people together. In order to have a better understanding of the term "culture," Stern suggests that writers "have tried to reduce the vast and amorphous nature of the culture concept to manageable proportions by preparing lists of items or by indicating a few broad categories" (208).

Stern in his Issues and Options in Language Teaching asserts the fact that there is a consensus on the objectives of teaching culture and indicates that the aims of this syllabus should be,

- To make one aware of the region of the learner or his/her own country.
- To develop acquaintance with the target culture.

- To develop an interest, intellectual curiosity and empathy.
- To become acquainted with the characteristics and differences between their and the target culture.
- To recognize the socio-cultural implications of language and language use.

2.7 SKILL-BASED APPROACH

Skills are capabilities that people must be able to do to be proficient enough in a language, rather independently of the circumstances or context in which the language use can occur. The content of the language teaching includes a compilation of specific skills that may play a role in using language in this syllabus. Though situational syllabi unite functions together into specific settings of language use, skill-based syllabi merge linguistic competencies (pronunciation, vocabulary, grammar, and discourse) together into universal types of behavior, such as listening to spoken language for the central idea, writing well-formed paragraphs, delivering effective lectures, and so forth. The important rationale behind skill-based instruction is to learn the specific language skill. The insignificant objective might be to develop more general competence in the language, learning only incidentally any sort of information that may be accessible while utilizing the language skills.

2.8 CONTENT-BASED APPROACH

Content-based syllabus proposes to design a type of instruction in which the central goal is to impart specific information and content along with the language that the learners are learning. Even though the subject matter is of primary and vital importance, language learning takes place concurrently with the content learning.

The students are at the same time language learners of whatever content and information is being taught. When compared with the task-based approach of language teaching that is concerned with communicative and cognitive processes, content-based language teaching deals with information. Content-based language teaching is associated with information. Any content subject like mathematics, computer, electronics or social sciences can be taught in the class with the linguistic adjustment more clearly.

2.9 MULTI-DIMENSIONAL APPROACH

The term Multi-dimensional indicates that it is possible to design a syllabus involving lessons of varying orientation: for instance, some including significant functions, others dealing with situations and topics, and yet others with notions and structures, as there is no serious rationale behind the selection of only one of the constructed item types as the unit of organization. The fundamental principle is that there should be flexibility to modify the central point of the teaching material as the course unfolds. This will lead to a syllabus design which is flexible, less rigid and more responsive to the student's choice of language needs.

2.10 LEXICAL APPROACH

Lexical approach emphasizes abstract concepts without reference to the words in a sentence. Willis says:

> ... taking lexis as a starting point enabled us to identify the commonest meanings and patterns in English, and to offer students a picture which is typical of the way English is used. (129-130)

He went ahead to claim that they were able to go behind the work of Wilkins and his contemporaries in their attempt to establish a notional syllabus. They were able to suggest to learners a way of referencing the language they had experienced. Therefore learners were able to use their corpus in the same way as grammarians and lexicographers employ a corpus in order to make valid and appropriate generalizations about the language under study.

Particularly, Willis' lexical syllabus is firmly based on real language. It offers some insights into that content which modifies and outlines the way syllabus designers treat the language in the course books. Hence the representation of the language one pictures in designing such a syllabus is quite different from what one might present intuitively. Indeed, intuition on its own cannot identify the most frequent words and phrases of the language, or even identify their importance. Previously the course writer's reliance on intuition has resulted in misrepresentations in the handling of the language. This lexical syllabus is strictly based on a body of research into natural language rather than other pedagogic grammars. The effect is to put forward a more complete pedagogic depiction of the language and a better balanced description as well.

One of the most important features of designing such a syllabus is the shifting of responsibility for learning onto the learner. Instead of offering discrete patterns to the learner, it facilitates the learner to familiarize with a corpus of language which is in many ways characteristic of the language as a whole. The learner learns from investigating and analyzing this corpus. Focusing the learners on carefully selected language, and by arming them with analyzing that language on their own, the syllabus helps the learners to successfully achieve their goals. Specifically speaking, it is a matter of dynamic thinking in the learner's creativity. Certainly by exploiting the creativity, the learning is vastly made more efficient.

2.11 LEARNER-LED APPROACH

Breen and Candlin were the first ones who proposed to base an approach on the belief of how learners learn. The learner is vital, who it is hoped will be involved in the accomplishment of the syllabus design as far as practically possible. The learners' knowledge and responsiveness of the course they are studying helps them enhance their interest and motivation, attached with the positive effect of developing the skills mandatory to learn.

This syllabus cannot be predetermined and prearranged. The syllabus design will be the responsibility of the learners and teachers. The critics of this view indicate that a learner-led syllabus seems far-reaching and radical, but it will be complicated to follow. Furthermore, without the support of a course book, a lack of aims also may occur.

2.12 PROPORTIONAL APPROACH

The proportional syllabus mainly tries to develop an overall proficiency of the learners. This syllabus is a blend of structural and functional elements. It appears appropriate and applicable for students who lack exposure to the target language beyond the classroom.

Infact, this syllabus comprises of a variety of elements with theme playing a linking part through the units. This theme is selected by the learners. Foremost, the form is of essential value, but later the emphasis will turn towards interactional elements. The change from form to interaction can occur at any time and is not limited to a particular level of student ability.

Yalden says it is important for a syllabus to indicate unambiguously "what will be taught, not what will be learned" (87). The leading view in designing a proportional syllabus centers around the principle that a syllabus has to indicate explicitly what will be taught, rather than what will be learned. Ultimately, the rationale behind designing such a syllabus is to develop a type of syllabus that is dynamic with abundant opportunity for feedback and flexibility.

2.13 ESP

English for Specific Purposes is considered as Learner-centered approach. It meets the needs of learners who need to learn a foreign language for use in their specific fields, such as science, technology, medicine, travel, and academic learning. The term 'specific' in ESP refers to the specific purpose for learning English. ESP development began as an answer to a surge in perceived language needs which came in the wake of a dramatic growth in science, industry and commerce in 1950s. English Language Teaching involves equipping the students with the "… basic ability of using English to receive and convey information regarding their specialist studies" (Allen and Widdowson). English teaching currently needs to provide students with the knowledge of how to achieve communicative purpose through various rhetorical devices and text genres. "It is important to move beyond the sentence level in our conceptions of grammar and focus on discourse" (Canale 27). This can be done only through a special curriculum designed specially for the purpose. Howatt says that since the 1960s, English for specific purposes (ESP) has become a vital and innovative activity in the teaching of English as a Foreign/Second language. ESP is regarded as an "approach", not as a "product" (Hutchinson & Waters 51). This approach desires to language teaching in which all decisions as to content and method depend on the learner's reason for learning. The needs analysis determine which language skills are preferred by the students, and the syllabus is designed accordingly.

In recent years, much emphasis has been given to information from and about learners. Assumptions about the learner's purpose in undertaking a language course, as well as the syllabus designer's beliefs about the nature of language and learning have a prominent influence on the outline of the syllabus on which the course is based. Learners' needs will vary according to how specific these are, and how instantly they wish to make use of their developing language skills. Methods and techniques for collecting information, which is to be used in syllabus design, are referred to as needs analysis. According to Nunan:

> In needs analysis, the analysts not only collect information about why learners want to learn the language, but also information about such things as social expectation, and teaching/learning constraints, and the resources available for implementing the programme. (13)

2.13.1 General English - ESP

The expansion of trade, commerce, economy and the continuing increase of global communication in various fields have lead to the demand for soft skills/inter personal skills/employability skills, particularly in countries where English is taught. Hence the key element in achieving success in one's career is by possessing the required communication skills. Potential employers are seeking a combination of skills in their new recruitments. They in addition to technical knowledge look for managerial skills which include communicative and human relations skills.

General English provides a broad foundation rather than a detailed and specification of goals like ESP Widdowson in learning purpose and language use distinguish General English and English for Specific Purposes. He says that i) In GE the focus is on education, whereas ESP focuses on training. ii) In General English, the future English needs are not taken into consideration. It will not predict the future needs; hence it is difficult to select course content. But for ESP it is easy to select course content as it predicts the purpose. iii) GE has varied age group learners and focuses generally on four skills: on Listening, Speaking, Reading and Writing. In contrast ESP is based on needs analysis that determines specific functional language skills. Based on the above, it can be said that the distinguishing aspects of ESP and General English are found in syllabus, materials and methodology.

ESL - ESP

'English as a second language' refers to when English happens to be the language of instruction in schools or as it is lingua franca among the speakers of widely diverse languages, as in India.

ESL and ESP are distinguished not only in the nature of the learning, but also in the aim of instruction. Indeed, as a general rule, while in ESL all four macro skills listening, reading, speaking, and writing are stressed, in ESP students usually learn the language to communicate in academic setting, to perform particular job-related functions. Therefore ESP is taught for the functions assessment of purposes, needs and the functions for which English is required.

ESP gives attention to the language in context than on teaching grammar and language structures. It covers subjects varying from accounting or computer science to engineering and business management. Its focal point is that English is not taught as a subject alienated from the students' real world; instead, it is integrated into the subject matter area important to the learners. Thus the approach is highly motivating because students are able to apply what they learn in their class rooms to their main field of study, whether it be mathematics, business management, economics, computer science or technology. Learners' knowledge of grammar, vocabulary and structures reinforces what is taught and increases their motivation.

2.13.2 ESP: Definition

Brumfit defines ESP as "...a course directly concerned with the purposes for which learners need English, purposes which are usually expressed in functional terms" (7). It is observed that ESP is congruent with the aims of communicative language teaching of recent times. The students' abilities in their subject fields, in turn, improve their ability to acquire English. Content subjects' knowledge gives them the context they need to understand the English of the classroom. In the learner-centered class, students are taught how the subject-matter is expressed in English.

Dudely Evans defines ESP in terms of 'absolute' and 'variable' characteristics. They are as follows:

Absolute Characteristics

1. ESP is defined to meet specific needs of the learners.
2. ESP makes use of underlying methodology and activities of the discipline it serves.
3. ESP is concerned with the language appropriate to these activities in terms of grammar, lexis, register, study skills, discourse and genre.

Variable Characteristics

1. ESP may be related to or designed for specific disciplines.
2. ESP may use, in specific teaching situations, a different methodology from that of General English.
3. ESP is likely to be designed for adult learners, either at tertiary level or in professional work situation.
4. ESP is designed for intermediate or advanced students.
5. Most ESP courses assume some basic knowledge of the language systems. (4)

Evidently, ESP is geared towards equipping the learners with the strategic ability to communicate effectively in a new situation, which they may encounter. It equips the learners with the "underlying competence" required to negotiate meaning.

2.13.3 Development of ESP Materials

Generally, English teachers depend on text books and available material which determine the content of the course. The text centers It is centered not only on the language (grammar, lexis, register), but also on the skills, discourses and genres. ESP evaluates needs and integrates subject matter and language for the teaching of relevant skills.

Usually designing material for ESP courses takes cognizance of the following facts:

- Linguistic and communicative competence needed at the end of the course.
- Diagnosis of the learners' linguistic problems.
- Selection of the course material.
- Identifying teaching elements — syntactic and semantic features (grammar, lexis, register) and skills.
- Appropriate discourse and genres.
- Methods and techniques appropriate in teaching the language.

2.14 ENGLISH FOR SCIENCE AND TECHNOLOGY

In case of EST, it is ridiculous to select a prose lesson or poetry that is recommended for literature or general students. The language course material chosen for Technical students must be relevant to the technical field. The language course material should possess technical register of the specific field. At the same time it may not be subject specific completely. It should be designed to cover the high frequency technical terminology and should systematically impart the grammar used in the field. The material can be selected from the relevant science and technology books.

2.14.1 Needs of the Learners

A student of Science and Technology needs English language for the following functions:

- To comprehend Technical subject during the lectures as well as in reading the books.
- To read reference books on technical subjects and prepare notes on his own.
- To give oral/written instructions.
- To write laboratory manuals/project reports etc.
- To present the known technical subject in the examination.
- To present the project topic orally.
- To discuss the subject with other persons.

The student should be able to achieve the following goals by the end of the course:

- To do well in the selection process for jobs in Technical, HR and Communication rounds.
- To handle the work on job independently and in teams.

2.14.2 Diagnosis of the learners' linguistic problems:

After knowing the needs and objectives of the learners, which are usually similar in ESP courses it is important for a language teacher to diagnose the linguistic problems of the pupils. i.e. their competence in grammar, lexis, register and discourse appropriate to their field. For example — in case of Engineering students a language teacher has to test the learners.

- Ability to use the technical terminology in the concerned field.
- Ability to use to describe the technical subject. Usually the syntax is very limited. For example, one tense i.e. using present tense in active form and passive form is enough. The language teacher has to test the pupils as to whether they can construct sentences properly to present their technical subject information in written or oral form.
- The language teacher for EST may test the students' language skills in reading, spelling, writing in the initial stage, because the students at the entry level usually have these problems.

2.14.3 Identifying the teaching elements

For imparting language skills in the EST course the language teacher has to identify the teaching elements from a linguistic point of view. The language teacher has to trace the register, lexis and syntax to be taught in the class rather than concentrating on the subject matter.

2.14.4 Syntax of the EST

Imperative sentences in Active voice & Passive voice.	v+obj/compl, ob+is/am/are/was/were+v3.
Sentences of the technical subject usually in simple present tense both in active and passive form	Sub + v1/v1+s/+es+obj/compl, Obj + is/are/am +v3........
Linking words of cumulative, contrasting, relative conjunctions	And, both, not only but also, as well as/ but, yet, however, still, despite/ either or, neither nor

2.5 CONCLUSION

These various syllabi touched upon offer valuable insights into creating a language course. Syllabi are frequently combined in more or less integrated ways with one type as the systematic starting point around which the others are arranged and connected. Indeed in arguing about syllabus choice and design, it must be taken into consideration that the question is not which type to select but which types and how to connect them with each other. Eventually, and perhaps preferably, a combination syllabus needs to be constructed and designed due to pragmatic reasons. It is obvious that no single type of syllabus is appropriate for all teaching settings. Because of the fact that the requirements and conditions of each setting are so characteristic and idiosyncratic that exact proposals for integration are not easily possible. The exploration on how subtly and carefully a syllabus can be developed and implemented opens a new horizon for future research.

CHAPTER 3

Communicative Language Teaching

The Communicative Language teaching emerged in ELT to attend the needs of learners. Linguists' views and observations proclaim that CLT focuses on functional English which is learner-centered. Sauvignon cites Montaigne's words on his learning of Latin through conversation. Montaigne writes, "Without methods, without a book, without grammar or rules, without a whip and without tears, I had learned Latin as proper as that of my schoolmaster" (47).

For some it is nothing but an integration of grammatical and functional teaching. Littlewood says, "One of the most characteristic features of communicative language teaching is that it pays systematic attention to functional as well as structural aspects of language" (1). Berns describes CLT as, "language teaching is based on a view of language as communication, that is, language is seen as a social tool which speakers use to make meaning; speakers communicate about something to someone for some purpose, either orally or in writing"(104). However the primary function of a language is for interaction and communication. Canale and Swain define CLT as, "with respect to teaching methodology, it is crucial that classroom activities reflect, in the most optimally direct manner, those communication activities that the learner is most likely to engage in… Furthermore, communication activities must be as meaningful as possible and be characterized (at increasing levels of difficulty) by aspects of genuine communication such as its basis in social interaction, the relative creativity and unpredictability of utterances, its purposefulness and goal-orientation, and its authenticity"(33).

Communicative Language Teaching emphasizes that the goal of language teaching is communicative competence. Thus CLT is an "approach that aims to (a) make competence the goal of language teaching and (b) develop procedures for teaching of the four language skills that acknowledge the interdependence of language and communication" (Richards and Rodgers 66).

Munby pointed out that competence is "the mastery of the abstract system of rules by which a person is able to understand and produce the well-formed sentences of his language" (7). But many sociolinguists argue that linguistic system alone is not enough for effective communication.

CLT is considered by some others as teaching authentic language. They say that authentic language communication involves the negotiation of meaning between speakers. Negotiation of meaning happens when some form of information exchange takes place for a real purpose. This makes the context of communication as relevant as the content (Nunan, 1998; Harmer, 2006). It means using procedures where learners work in pairs/groups, using their language resources to problem-solving tasks.

Direct practice of communicative acts, focus on socio-cultural contexts, curriculum based on experience have become central to CLT. CLT today is seen as an approach-Communicative Approach- and not a method. It aims to make communicative competence the goal of language teaching and develop procedures for the teaching of the four skills that acknowledge the interdependence of language and communication.

This chapter looks into the significance of Communicative language teaching/learning processes. It is divided into two sections. Section A deals with Communication skills through LSRW and Section B looks at CALL, CLL and TBLT.

I. Communication skills through Listening, Speaking, Reading, Writing (LSRW)

3.1 INTRODUCTION

Communicative approach is widely used to teach English in Engineering colleges today as the demand for English speaking and listening has increased due to globalization. Listening competence is necessary for the aspirants to take the tests like Test of English and Foreign Languages (TOEFL), Graduate Record Examination (GRE) which make teaching 'listening' a priority. Reading and writing take next place to listening and speaking. Reading skill is indispensable for reading academic subjects and for information. Students need to write a lot as job seekers and as employees. In today's world of technology, it is mandatory to

know the writing of Resumes, Curriculum Vitae (CV), Letter Writing, E-Correspondence, E mail writing, Report writing etc. Teaching/Learning communication skills means Teaching/Learning the four macro skills: LSRW. These four basic skills are complexly related to each other in receiving and producing a message.

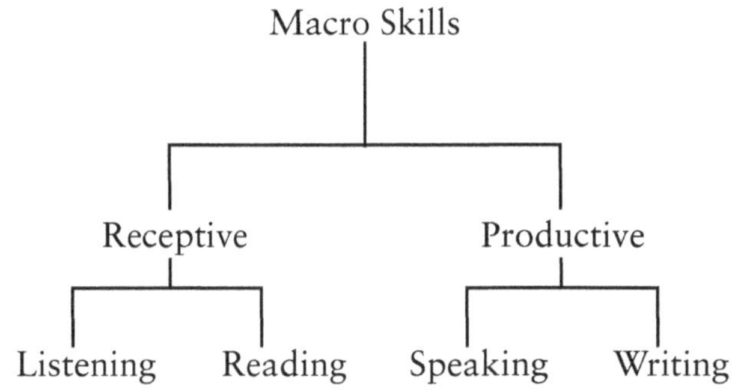

3.2 LISTENING

Among the macro skills of language learning, listening is the most consequential communication skill. However, it is relegated to a lesser role in many educational institutions. Listening is the responsiveness to information. The organization of information entering the nervous system via the hearing mechanism. Contrary to hearing, which is a physiological passive activity, listening is an active cognitive process. The process of listening begins with hearing. Hearing occurs when ears pick up sound waves which are then transported to brain. This stage is sense of hearing. Hearing is an impromptu act. Listening requires not only to hear what has been said but to understand as well. Understanding requires concentration and attention. It is obvious that language learning depends on listening. It provides the aural input that serve as the basis for language acquisition and allows learners to interact in spoken communication.

According to Howatt and Dakin (1974), listening is the ability to identify and understand what is said by others. This process involves understanding a speaker's accent or pronunciation, the speaker's grammar and vocabulary, and comprehension of meaning.

Thomlinson in his paper "Public Relations and Listening" says that, "active listening," goes beyond comprehending or understanding the message content, to an act of empathetic understanding of the speaker. Furthermore, Gordon (1985) argues that empathy is essential to listening and contends that it is more than a polite attempt to identify a speaker's perspectives.

Keith Davies in his book, *Human Behaviour at Work*, says that "Hearing is with the ears, but listening is with the mind" (385). Listening is the fundamental among the macro skills. Through this medium of transmitting the language people gain a lot in their education. It differs person to person in receiving the information, their perception of the world. It is evident that without listening skills the students will not acquire anything.

The theory of second language acquisition stresses upon language input which is the most essential condition of language acquisition. As listening is receptive input skill, it plays a crucial role in students' language development. Krashen (1985) argues that people acquire language by understanding the linguistic information they hear. Thus language acquisition is achieved mainly through receiving input. Given the importance of listening in language learning, it is essential for language teachers to help students become effective listeners. The learner-centered communicative approach to language teaching, focuses on modelling listening techniques and providing listening practice in authentic situations; precisely those situations. The learners are likely to encounter when they use the language outside the classroom.

3.2.1 Strategies of listening comprehension

The listener uses certain techniques or activities that contribute directly to the comprehension and recall of listening input. Depending on the way the listener processes the input, the listening comprehension is divided into two approaches

In the Listener-based approach the listener adopts Tope-down strategies where one is acquainted with the listener jump into background knowledge of the topic, the situation or context, the type of text and the language. The information of background knowledge activates a set of expectations that help the listener to interpret the speech and predict what will come next.

The Strategies used here:
- Looking for the main idea
- Predicting
- Drawing inferences
- Summarizing

In the text based approach, the listener adopts Bottom-up strategies where the listener depends on the language in the message, which means the combination of sounds, words and grammar which create meaning.

The Strategies used here:
- Looking for specific details
- Distinguishing cognates
- Identifying word-order patterns

Listening comprehension is inclined to be an interactive, interpretive process in which listeners use prior awareness and linguistic knowledge in understanding messages. Listeners use the strategies of metacognitive (learners' automatic awareness of their own knowledge and their ability to understand), cognitive (mental process of knowing. This would include, thinking, reasoning, perception, awareness, and judgment) and socio-affective strategies (emotions, attitudes and the relations to the society) to facilitate comprehension and to make their learning more effective. Metacognitive strategies are important because they regulate and direct the language learning process. Research shows that skilled listeners use more metacognitive strategies than their less-skilled counterparts (O'Malley & Chamot 1990, Vandergrift 1997).

3.2.2 Distractions from listening

Noise of all kinds.

- Language problems, various accents which are not familiar.
- Physical problems like stammer, illness, hearing difficulties, mental conditions.
- Anxiety, fear, emotional upset.

Though these problems distract from listening, one can be an active listener by adopting good listening strategies.

3.2.3 Useful listening strategies

It is important to identify why and what the speaker is saying. One may be an unmotivated listener if there is no reason for listening to the speaker.

- The listener should not blame the speaker by being passive or unattentive. It depends on the listener to be responsible and to understand.
- Noise may distract from listening. It is better to be away from sources of human or mechanical noises.
- Listener has to make sure of what the speaker is saying before rejecting.
- It is advisable to ask the speaker to repeat or tell more about something if it is not clear.
- It is a wise act to identify the speaker's pattern of organization. In a lecture, a speaker may refer to notes or some other source of information.
- Identifying the main idea of the presentation and distinguishing between the important and trivial is crucial.
- It is not necessary to talk more to sustain a healthy relationship with the customer. Often skillful listening is more valuable than talking.

- The tendency of taking position at every opening in conversation may eliminate many of the potential benefits of listening. The speaker may not feel good, whose thinking and brainstorming will be inhibited and may even hold back important information out of caution or annoyance.
- The speaker must be put at ease. Disturbing the speaker by giving suggestions prevent's the speaker's flow of speech.
- While attending employment interviews, applicants need to be attentive listeners in order to develop a good rapport with their interviewers and gain impression within a limited amount of time.

Lesikar and Flately has proposed certain listening strategies:

- Put the speaker at ease.
- Show the speaker that you are interested in listening to him. Then the speaker gives his best.
- Remove distractions. Listener's idle behaviors like shuffling papers, scribbling etc. would distract both.
- Patience of the listener allows the speaker take his own time to make his point without hurrying.
- Control temper at any provocation from the speaker. Take it easy on criticism and argument (407- 408).

To become a better listener one has to practice "active listening." This is where one makes a conscious effort to hear not merely the words that another person is saying but, more importantly, to try and comprehend the total message being sent.

However, careful observation of College English teaching has found that the instruction on Listening skills is still the weak link in the language teaching process. Despite students having mastered the basic elements of English grammar and vocabulary, their listening comprehension needs to be improved.

3.3 SPEAKING SKILLS

The productive skill, speaking is like the other skills, but is more complex than it seems, as it is not merely pronouncing the words. Speaking in academic contexts is becoming increasingly important as students are required to participate in group work and joint projects. Speaking and writing in academic setting are similar in many ways: they are linear, formal, explicit, hedged and responsible. They have one central point and are presented in standard language. However speaking is objective and is less complex than written language.

3.3.1 The following factors are important in the speaking process

- Pronunciation is the most important aspect in speaking because mispronunciation sends wrong message to the listener. Hence pronounce the distinctive sounds of a language clearly enough so that people can distinguish them.
- To make the listener comfortable with the speech, use intonation, stress and rhythm patterns of the language.
- Clarity is achieved if the correct forms of words are used (changes in the tense, case, or gender) and correct word order is maintained.
- Appropriate vocabulary adds clarity and richness to the expression.
- Use of appropriate register or language variety suitable to the situation and the relationship with the conversation partner.
- To make the listener understand the main sentence constituents, such as subject, verb, object etc.

- To construct the main ideas to stand out from supporting ideas or information.
- To craft the discourse to hang together so that people can follow what one is saying.

3.3.2 Functional English

Functional English prepares the students with the necessary knowledge, skills and understanding to apply English language in everyday life like; presenting information, to engage in conversation with others confidently, solving problems in familiar and unfamiliar situations, summarizing information, persuading others etc. Functional English ensures correct usage of English in day to day life.

Learning various speech patterns, phrases, formal and informal speaking, assuming the situations in everyday social and professional interaction help master the speaking skills. Students can practice these functions of the language; advising and persuading, agreeing and apologizing, asking for clarification, asking for information, asking for opinion, asking for permission, challenging, challenging the subject, classifying, comparing, concluding, checking whether people are following, description of graphs and figures, description of objects, description of procedures, description of processes and developments and changes, emphasizing a point, giving examples, expressing method and means, expressing certainty, expressing reasons and explanations, giving background information, further information, instructions, opinions, preventing the interruption, listing, narrating, presenting results, referring to research, quoting directly, requesting, rephrasing sequencing, summarizing etc.

3.3.3 Presentation skills

In addition to basic functional English it is very essential to learn speaking in an academic context for making presentations and taking part in discussions.

3.3.4 To make an effective presentation one should

- Know the purpose of the seminar and know the audience
- Introduce the topic giving information in detail
- Take care in sequencing; describing similarities and differences, comparing and contrasting while illustrating a point by giving examples; referring to research by emphasizing points etc.
- Control the discussion; lead the discussion; keep the audience involved
- Change the subject
- Move on to a new point
- Emphasize important points
- Speed up things
- Make suggestions
- Prevent interruptions
- Summarise and conclude

3.4 READING SKILLS

3.4.1 Introduction

Reading is a process of receiving and interpreting the written word. It involves recognising what is written and comprehending the main and supplementary points as well as links between different parts of the material. The following reading techniques are helpful in understanding the text.

3.4.2 Types of Reading

3.4.2.1 Skimming

Based on the purpose of one's reading, techniques are used for better understanding. Skimming is a technique used to quickly identify the main ideas of a text. While reading a newspaper, one probably will not read word-by-word, but instead will scan the text. Skimming is done at a speed of three to four times from normal reading. When people want to read lots of material in a limited amount of time they adopt this technique. Some read the first and last paragraphs using headings, summarizes as they move down the page or screen. One might read the titles, subtitles, subheading and illustrations. The technique of reading is to get overall impression of the content.

3.4.2.2 Scanning

The reading technique of scanning is often used to check a word in the telephone book or dictionary. Searching for key words or ideas and in most cases one knows what he/she is looking for, by concentrating on finding a particular answer. Eyes move quickly down the page seeking specific words and phrases. This technique is also used when one first finds a resource to determine whether it will answer the questions. Once the document is scanned, one can go back and skim it. While scanning, one looks for the author's use of numbers, letters, steps, or the words first, second, or next etc. Indicators such as in the previous line or words that are bold faced, italicized, or in a different font size, style, color or the ideas in the margin communicate the essence of the text.

3.4.3 Reading strategies

Vocabulary

In order to understand any text, one needs to recognize the meaning of words as well as guess the meaning from word structure and infer the meaning from the context. To develop effective reading students should possess requisite vocabulary.

Translation/Inference:

The process of knowing the unknown from the known. For easier understanding one can read in one's own language first, and then read the same in English. Though there is new vocabulary, prior knowledge of information makes one guess what it is.

Prediction:

Students use their understanding of the text to determine what happens next, i.e. predicting by one's general knowledge.

3.4.4 Schema Theory of Reading

According to Cook the concept of schema is: "A representation of a typical instance which helps people to make sense of the word more quickly because people understand new experiences by activating relevant schema in their mind"(86). The concept of schema thus is the ability to comprehend and predict the situations, as the acquisition of knowledge activates the brain to respond and infer appropriately subsequent situations.

Though there is distinction among the readers of a text, they still share certain common traits in deriving the meaning as follows:

- Recognising the words
- The spelling and pronunciation
- Evaluating the meaning
- Grammatical functions
- Predicting the gist of the text
- Comprehending the coherence between sentences and paragraphs
- Understanding the ambiguity
- Applying personal knowledge to comprehend the implied and unrevealed
- Distinguishing the tone of the author, the purpose of writing the text
- Contemplating the background of the text
- Understanding the time, the way of the world in a particular period through the text

3.4.5 Types of Reading

3.4.5.1 Top-Down Reading

Top-down strategy focuses on the learner's knowledge obtained earlier, which causes improving language learning and reading comprehension. According to Carrel "Reading is a receptive language process, in that it starts with a linguistic surface representation encoded by a writer and ends with the meaning which the reader constructs." He further says, "a lack of content schemata activation would lead to insurmountable processing difficulties with second language readers" (239-259).

Hudson has argued that "… a high degree of background knowledge can overcome linguistic deficiency. In addition to prior knowledge as a key point, top-down model is actually a whole-language teaching approach, in which readers focus on the context, and manage to construct meaning in the text" (32).

3.4.5.2 Bottom-Up Reading

In Bottom-Up reading the attention is paid to the written text than to the meaning. The readers observe only the spelling of the word. Grabe asserts that "the goals of the bottom-up approach are automatic word recognition and rapid reading rate, To reach the aims, explicit instruction in phonics and spelling is crucial; students should not be word-bound" (375).

3.5 WRITING SKILLS

3.5.1 Introduction

Writing is the most important means of communication within an organization. Maximum of work-time is engaged in written communication. Thus it is absolutely vital for a Professional Engineer to actively develop the skill of writing. Since much of the communication with superiors and the management occur in writing, one's whole career depends upon its quality. Writing Technical Reports, Memos, Official Letters, Resume writing, Email writing is part of writing skills.

3.5.2 Writing guidelines

Since writing is a powerful means of communication, one must be trained in writing effectively. To get the command over writing, it is essential to learn writing skills. Any written document must have structure, coherence and clarity in presenting the information so as to reach the reader.

3.5.2.1 Structure

The document can be broken into distinct sections, having in view the aim of writing and the reader; these sections are then further divided into subsections until arriving at simpler, smaller units of information which are expressed as a paragraph. Each paragraph in a document should justify itself; it should serve a purpose, or be removed. A paragraph should convey a single idea and can possess the following characteristics.

- Idea formation
- Elucidation or similarity
- Illustrations
- Use of sustaining evidences
- Contextual links to strengthen the structure

Engineers often use diagrams which make better sense than the written text. Reports can be written almost exclusively with them. Diagrams convey information more effectively and they often assist in the analysis and interpretation of the data. Using a pie chart gives a faster comparison than a list of numbers. By using a bar chart is far more comprehensible than the numbers it represents. By using informative labels and titles, key entries are highlighted and unnecessary information is removed.

3.5.2.2 Outline, Revise and Edit

While writing any draft one has to decide what to say, to whom, how to structure it and then check it for clarity. Keeping in mind the writing guidelines the written draft can be revised and edited.

3.5.2.3 The Beginning

The beginning of the document is crucial. It should be obvious to the reader at a glance about the document, and the purpose of it. It is necessary to catch the reader's attention and allow him/her deduce why it should be read. The document must not contain "teasing elevations of suspense."

3.5.2.4 Punctuation

Punctuation provides clarity to the draft, meaning and structure. It eliminates ambiguity. Hence tend not to punctuate, but for easy interpretation it is very much necessary.

3.5.2.5 Spelling

Spelling is a constant problem to some learners. It distracts the reader if incorrect spelling occurs frequently. One can take the assistance of computer spell-checking programmes, which is supported by a good dictionary. Chronic spellers should always maintain a (preferably alphabetical) list of corrected errors, and try to learn new rules (and exceptions). For instance (in British English) advice-advise, device-devise, license-license, practice-practice each follow the same pattern: the -ice is a noun, the -ise is a verb.

3.5.2.6 Length of a Sentence

Use of bombastic terminology and too many words instead of few may make the reader impatient. It would be wise to avoid long sentences. Generally a sentence is associated with a unit of information. Consequently the process of reading for information is extended till the full stop is reached. The reader is stopped at the long sentence and complex word. When the reader is distracted by the strange or complex word, then interest of reading will be lost and least attention is paid to the information conveyed. If the sentence is too long, one may lose the information because of limited attention span.

3.5.2.7 Jargon

It is appreciated if professional terminology is used when required. Irrelevant words lead to ambiguity. If one would like to write an impressive article, it is easy to slip into ostentatious way. Though the words and phrases sound significant, they convey nothing but noise.

3.5.3 Modern Writing- E-mails

Today every one uses e-mails to make requests, to answer questions, and to give announcements. E-mails can be read rapidly. Hence it would be better to get to the point in the first paragraph— the first sentence. Careful attention need to be shown regarding e-mails which make complaints. These are usually better handled in person.

Title of the e mail is important. Because the reader opens the title of e-mail in the 'Inbox' or in the folder where it has been stored, give some thought to the title. Writing a title orients the reader to the subject of the e-mail and, if possible, it distinguishes from other e-mails.

An email can be sent to one person or many at a time by writing their addresses in the box provided.

II: CALL, CLL & TBLT

Today when India has become a hot destination for multinationals, BPO jobs, outsourcing, and is also viewed as a hub for trained professionals in various fields, it is the students who are losing out despite their skill and expertise owing to a lack of communicative ability in English. Pondering over the dismal situation of ELT, various experts and linguists, teachers and trainers have come up with innovative and effective approaches. The methods that have gained widespread acceptance and mobility in contemporary times

are Computer Assisted Language Learning (CALL), Cooperative Language Learning (CLL) and Task Based Language Teaching (TBLT). The significance of the language laboratory has been much felt in the domain of communication. To train the students in Communication skills and Employability skills (which are synonymous to Soft skills/interpersonal skills/life skills/survival skills) a tension free environment is necessary in using the language, getting a feedback and an opportunity to correct the mistakes. A right platform to realize this purpose is Language Laboratory.

Cooperative Language Learning is seen as an extension of the principles of CLT. Learner is at the centre of this process. Cooperation among the learners is built by making them work in pairs or groups. The advanced learners help the weak learners and act as resources to them.

TBLT is student oriented and practical in approach, as distinguished from Text Based Learning. This approach equips the student with the required basic language skills. As students take part actively using the language in performing the tasks just as they do in a practical situation in life, it makes the learner equip himself with the required basic skills.

This section deals with two learner-centred language learning processes CALL, CLL and innovative teaching method TBLT.

3.6 COMPUTER ASSISTED LANGUAGE LEARNING (CALL)

Introduction

Scientific advancements have created innovative facilities to assist the learning process. It has extended its sophisticated products into the field of communication. Computers have revolutionized data storage and retrieval and added a new dimension to educational technology. Innovative products such as

Computers with net connection, LCD Projector, digital multimedia control, wireless headsets and microphones, the teacher's console to broadcast, public addressing system, etc. are practical and helpful for students learning languages for communication. It is useful to take note of the word "assisted" in CALL, which emphasizes that technology cannot replace the teacher in the classroom but can only lend assistance in learning.

3.6.1 Attributes of CALL

Computers can perform a variety of functions. However, Cook ascribes four aspects to CALL as follows. They are as follows:

- The computer can be used for creating timetables and planning courses.
- It can be used for testing.
- It can be used as a classroom aid.
- It can be used for direct teaching. (Cook 1985, 13)

3.6.2 The Theoretical Basis

Computer Assisted Language Learning is an emerging trend in language education. In spite of its discomfited beginning owing to lack of knowledge in usage of Computer technology in the language teaching community, it is growing as a powerful tool in the hands of experienced teachers. The multimedia computer provides the necessary most favorable input and practice activities.

The traditional class room is tedious to the learners in learning English. They are unmotivated and restrictive to meet their needs. Unless an effective practice is provided by well-designed course, the learning process becomes slow. Traditional language learning models give overemphasis for memorization and conscious learning of grammar rules that is soon forgotten. CALL creates learning environment by providing visual, auditory and related input in ways that a book cannot.

3.6.3 Language Laboratory

To acquire a sensibility for the sounds and rhythm of a language, one has to hear the best samples of a spoken language (Richards: 2001). The language laboratory is a very helpful tool for practicing and assessing one's speech. It provides a facility which allows the student to listen to model pronunciation, repeat and record the same, listen to their performance and compare with the model, and do self-assessment. Since the language laboratory gives every learner of any language freedom to learn at their own pace, it does not necessarily require a teacher all the time. At the same time, it is possible for teachers to provide assistance individually and collectively. The language course materials are already fed into the computer and are displayed according to the features available in the system. It allows every student his or her privacy to speak and listen. This is precisely the function of the language laboratory. Some highlights of the language laboratory are given below:

- It helps one to learn pronunciation, accent, stress and all other aspects of the phonetics of a language.
- It is a platform for learning functional English by Role Play, assuming world situations.
- It provides a chance to rehearse Oral Presentations and Technical Presentation.
- It gives chance to debate and have group discussions.
- Mock interview sessions can be organized.
- BBC News, Videos on the prescribed syllabus and others can be watched.
- Mock tests on international examinations like IELTS, TOEFL and other competitive examinations can be organized.

The electronic devices used in the laboratory will stimulate the eyes and ears of the learner to acquire the language quickly and easily. The laboratory's collection is designed to assist learners in the acquisition and maintenance of aural comprehension, oral and written proficiency, and cultural awareness. The language laboratory offers broadcasting, web-assisted materials and videotaped recordings in the target language. Hence, the language laboratory has become the need of the hour in any language learning process for communication. There is a wide range of on-line applications which are already available for use in the foreign language class. These include dictionaries and encyclopedias, blogs, links for teachers, pronunciation tutors, grammar and vocabulary quizzes, games and puzzles, literary extracts etc. The World Wide Web (WWW) is a virtual library of information that can be accessed by any user around the clock. If someone wants to read or listen to the news, for example, there are a number of sources offering the latest news either recorded or in printed form. The most important newspapers and magazines in the world are available on-line.

3.6.4 The Role of a Teacher in English Language Communication skills Lab

The teacher as a facilitator creates enthusiasm among the learners through innovative strategies. The teacher has to monitor and provide guidelines for learning. Most of the students lack basic knowledge of using a computer. The teacher should instruct them in learning. Based on the syllabus the teacher frames a variety of exercises for student's practice. In addition to the syllabus and the material, the teacher can prepare his/her own material (web resources) to update the learning process. The teacher should assign projects and motivate the students for their self learning by furnishing relevant websites.

CLT emphasizes different roles for teachers and learners which are quite different from the traditional L2 classrooms. Thus, Cook states that "The teacher is no longer a dominant figure continuously controlling and guiding the students. Rather the teacher takes one step back and lets the students take over their activities, making up their own conversations in pairs and groups, learning language by doing" (140). In the same way, the teacher can be a manager and organizer of classroom activities. "In this role, one of his/her major responsibilities is to establish situations likely to promote communication" (Larsen-Freeman 131), and "to organize the classroom as a setting for communication and communicative activities" (Richards and Rodgers 78). Knowles emphasizes the role of a teacher as, "A procedural technician, resource person and co-inquirer; he is more a catalyst than an instructor, more a guide than a wizard" (43).

3.6.5 Obstacles of Computer-assisted Language Learning:

- Financial barriers (establishing the Laboratory with well configured systems)
- Acceptance of the technology.
- Availability of computer hardware and software
- Technical and theoretical knowledge (Teachers should be familiar with the basic internet technology in order to anticipate potential problems. They should be able to avail online help resources.)

3.7 COOPERATIVE LANGUAGE LEARNING (CLL)

Cooperative language learning is an approach to language teaching that makes maximum use of cooperative activities including pairs and small groups of learners in the classroom. Olsen and Kagan define it as follows:

Cooperative learning is group learning activity organized so that learning is dependent on the socially structured exchange of information between learners in groups and in which each learner is held accountable for his or her own learning and is motivated to increase the learning of others. (8)

CLL is seen as an extension of the principles of CLT. It is viewed as a learner-centered approach and provides opportunities for naturalistic second language acquisition through the use of pair and group activities. CLL in the teaching context aims at the following:

- Raise the achievement of all the students, including gifted or academically handicapped.
- Helps the teacher build positive relationships among students.
- Give students the experiences they need for healthy social and psychological growth.
- Cognitive development replaces the competitive classroom with a team-based, high performance classroom. (Olsen and Kagan 1992: 8)

CLL as an approach fosters cooperation rather than competition, develops critical thinking skills and communicative competence through socially structured interactive activities.

From the perspective of second language teaching, McGroarty (1989) offers the following learning advantages for learners in CLL classrooms:

- Increased frequency and variety of second language practice through different types of interaction.
- Possibility for use of language in ways that support cognitive development and increased language skills.
- Opportunities to integrate language with content based instruction.

- Opportunities to include a greater variety of curricular materials to stimulate language as well as concept learning.
- Opportunities for students to act as resources for each other, thus assuming a more active role in their learning.

Olsen and Kagan (1992) propose the following key outcomes of successful group based learning.

- Positive interdependence
- Group formation
- Individual accountability
- Social skills

CLL is thus an approach that crosses both mainstream education and second language teaching.

3.8 TASK BASED LANGUAGE TEACHING (TBLT)

TBLT proposes the concept of "task" as a fundamental unit of planning and teaching. Although, definitions of task vary, a common understanding is that task is a goal that is carried out using language. The key assumptions of task-based instruction are summarized by Feez as:

- The focus is on process rather than product.
- Basic elements are purposeful activities and tasks that emphasize communication and meaning.
- Learners learn language by interacting communicatively and purposefully while engaged in the activities and tasks.
- Activities and tasks can be either—those that the learners might need to achieve in real life; those that have a pedagogical purpose specific to the classroom.
- Activities and tasks are sequenced according to the level of difficulty.

- The difficulty of a task depends on a range of factors including the previous experience of the learner, the complexity of the task, the language required to undertake a task, and the degree of support available. (17)

Task Based Language Teaching (TBLT) is an approach which offers learners material which they employ actively in order to attain a goal or complete a task. A great deal of regular tasks that are performed each day such as making tea, writing an essay, talking to someone on the phone etc. can be the material. TBLT looks for the development of students' interlanguage by providing a task and then using language to solve it.

Linguistic competence and Communication skills imparted to the students through well defined course structure may also ignore the target of improving communicative ability of the learner unless their knowledge is put into practical use. Tasks should be integrated into the language syllabi based on the needs, requirements and with the knowledge of the learner in mind. Most of the students are incapable of filling up simple documents of various offices like filling up a bank pay in slip or Demand Draft, Pass port application or various other applications. These tasks can be done by the students as part of their project work. The aim of a Task is to enhance the ability of the learner to acquire and produce meaning rather than form.

According to Nunan, Task Based Learning gives more prominence to meaning than to the grammatical form. He states,

A piece of classroom work that involves learners in comprehending, manipulating, producing or interacting in the target language [English] while their attention is focused on mobilizing their grammatical knowledge in order to express meaning, and in which the intention is to convey meaning rather than to manipulate form.

The task should also have a sense of completeness, being able to stand alone as a communicative act in its own right with a beginning, middle and an end. (Nunan 4)

While implementing TBL in classrooms in our country the level of the students and the situation; topics that the learners' can relate to; aims to be achieved and most importantly tasks to be designed are to be remembered.

TBL needs a certain degree of previous knowledge and a lot of planning. Before carrying out the task, it has to be well defined in addition to the suggestions and clues to perform the task. The knowledge as well as the expected outcome or result needs to be predicted, defined and communicated to the students before taking the task. Those who take the task should be clear as how they are required to execute the task so as to achieve the pre-defined outcome. TBL can be implemented in three stages.

1. Pre-Task Stage

The primary step of a task is to plan and provide required inputs to the students and implement. The teacher explains the task to the students by giving clues to execute the task properly. The tasks can be demonstrated either by teacher or with the aid of the computer (videos) for better understanding. The teacher has to explain the expected outcome of the task so that the student can work in the right direction. According to the task design it can be an individual activity, group activity, class activity or home activity.

2. Task Stage

The task stage comprises of the student performing the task as determined in the prior stage. The role of the teacher is crucial here to observe and act as a facilitator and counselor to the student.

According to the guidelines, the students enact the tasks to achieve the outcome. They chalk out the strategies for presentation of the result in the form of presentation, report or discussion.

3. Post-Task Stage

This stage assesses the outcome of the task. Task can be repeated by identifying the mistakes for rectifying. The task has to be evaluated through discussion.

The teacher gives feedback on the performance, their mistakes, and problem areas and endeavors to overcome the obstacles to effective communication and language learning that they are facing.

3.8.1 Features of TBLT

Motivation:

Tasks should tickle the student's mind into alertness and raise his curiosity to perform.

Learner Centered:

The students learn in a friendly environ rather than by listening to serious lectures. The students take active role in performing tasks. The teacher acts as the facilitator or instructor or counselor. Hence the teaching process becomes learner centered.

Teacher and Student relation:

Good rapport is established particularly in the pre and post task stages by means of their respective interactive sessions on planning and preparation. After the completion of tasks the teacher and the learners should work on evaluation, assessment and correction because the teacher gives feedback and the learners have to listen and correct themselves.

Form of Language:

A paradigm shift in today's ELT scenario is the importance given to the meaning rather than grammatical form. Here students learn to use language form more completely drawing on their latent knowledge of form and grammar in a meaningful context.

Practical Language Usage:

Tasks are mainly based on practical application of the language that enhances the learner's ability to use their linguistic skill in real life situations and context.

Communication:

TBLT is based on a Communicative approach to ELT. It develops the verbal and non-verbal ability and communicative skills of the learners practically.

Comprehension:

Due to the priority of meaning in TBL, the level of comprehension is enhanced among the students. The tasks must be clear to the learner in order to be executed properly, which finally leads to a comprehensible and complete outcome.

Spontaneity:

Tasks engage individual or group activity which needs spontaneous thinking and execution on the part of the students. Learners must be active to understand and execute the task, which also develops their thinking power.

Group Interaction:

The form of task that is incorporated involves group interface as a part of the pre-task, task or post-task phase in the form of discussion, evaluation, repetition etc.

Confidence:

As soon as the learner performs a task successfully it raises his level of confidence upon his accomplishment. This further gives an impetus to the learning process as well as to his communicative ability and skill.

Decision Making:

Since a task involves multiple choices, it develops the decision making ability of the students. The student has to decide how and in what way he will perform the task, thereby choosing from the set of options before him.

Independence:

The students are active in TBL class, the role of teacher is relatively passive in the task process. This improves the quality of independence amongst the students encouraging them to think and communicate independently.

3.8.2 Tasks that can be conducted on LSRW

Listening
- Sounds (phonetics)
- Comprehension
- Stories

Speaking
- Just a minute/extempore
- Role Play
- Debate/Group Discussion
- Interview

Reading
- Comprehension
- Stories
- Vocabulary
- Analogies

Writing
- Paragraphs
- Letters
- Reports/Memos
- Emails

TBLT's topics for the tasks to be performed in the laboratory should be close to a student's life and interest, and also those that he/she can relate to without much difficulty.

3.9 CONCLUSION

To master the language, the students must have the foundation with the basics of LSRW skills and functional English. CALL, CLL and TBLT allow the student to learn through practical means and at their own pace which make learning processes profitable. The communicative approach is advantageous for both teaching and learning process as it brings out the intrinsic motivational strengths of learners, fosters student interest, and encourages behavioural and attitudinal change and provides opportunities for success.

CHAPTER 4

Framework of Current Syllabi

4.1 INTRODUCTION

A course book is looked upon as an obligatory means for foreign language acquisition whose validity and significance are hardly ever questioned. Students feel secure and have a sense of progress and achievement with a course book. They would like to have a book to relate to; otherwise their journey of the study programme is groping in the dark. Therefore, they become more confident and satisfied, as they tackle the target language within a certain framework. In addition, a textbook provides them with the opportunity to go back and revise, for self-study and as a reference tool. Moreover, a well-illustrated book, equipped with the necessary contents caters to the needs of the students. The teachers as facilitators play a crucial role in instructing the students with innovative methods.

Section 'A' deals with the English Course designed by JNTU for the Engineering students. English is offered twice. In the I year of the programme a full course is offered. Keeping in view the needs and requirements of the outgoing students of the Engineering programme an Advanced English course is offered for a semester in the III/IV year.

Section B outlines the English course offered for the students of Engineering colleges which come under the purview of the Kakatiya University.

SECTION A

4.2 COURSE DESIGN OF I YEAR B.TECH ENGLISH, J.NT.U.

JNTU syllabus designers make clear in the manual that the growing importance of English as a tool for global communication and the consequent emphasis on training students to acquire communicative competence has made them to design the Syllabus to develop linguistic and communicative competence of the students.

4.2.1 To achieve the above objective, JNTU had prescribed the following books:

These books are prescribed in the year 2007.

Detailed study: *Enjoying Everyday English, ed*. Ramakrishna Rao A, Sangam Books, Hyderabad.

Non-detailed study: *Inspiring Speeches and Lives ed*. Yadava Raju and Murali Krishna, Maruthi Publications, Guntur.

J.N.T.U. supplied an instruction manual *Academic Regulations, Course Structure and Detailed Syllabus* which serves as a guide to the teacher with an introduction to the course, objectives of the course and the time frame for the teaching of the units of the prescribed syllabus.

Describing the way the detailed and non-detailed texts are to be used, the framers say:

In the English classes, the focus should be on the skills of reading, writing, listening and speaking and for this the teachers should use the text prescribed for detailed study. For example, the students should be encouraged to read the texts/selected paragraphs silently. The teachers can ask comprehension questions to stimulate discussion and based on the discussions students can be made to write short paragraphs/essays etc. (Manual 21)

The text for non-detailed study is for extensive reading/reading for pleasure by the students. Hence, it is suggested that they read it on their own with topics selected for discussion in the class. The time should be utilized for working out the exercises given after each section, as also for supplementing the exercises with authentic materials of a similar kind for example, from newspaper articles, advertisements, promotional material etc. However, the stress in this syllabus is on skill development and practice of language skills.

The detailed and the non-detailed texts are accompanied by audio CDs. The CD for the detailed text *Enjoying Everyday English* has listening and speaking materials related to the corresponding sections in the book and also supplementary, interactive exercises in grammar and vocabulary. The non-detailed text *Inspiring Speeches and Lives* is accompanied by a video CD. The CD shows four speeches being delivered. The prescribed texts and exercises are meant to serve broadly as students' handbooks.

In addition to the above, the manual *Academic Regulations Course Structure and Detailed Syllabus* gives a list of books to be used for reference by the teachers and students. The following is the list:

4.2.2 The following is the list of reference books as given by the framers

- English Grammar in Steps – D. Bolton and N. Goodey
- English Grammar Practice – R.N. Bakshi
- Expressway to English – B.K. Das
- Intermediate Grammar and Composition – K.R. Narayanaswamy
- Spoken English: A Foundation Course – K. Sadanand and S. Punitha
- Strengthen Your Writing -.R. Narayanaswami

4.2.3 Objectives of the Syllabus

The manual *Academic Regulations, Course Structure and Detailed Syllabus* deals exhaustively with the objectives of the course offered. The following are the objectives outlined in the manual in pages 21-23.

General Objectives

1. To improve the language proficiency of the students in English with emphasis on LSRW (Listening, Speaking, Reading, Writing) skills.
2. To equip the students to study academic subjects with greater facility through the theoretical and practical components of the English syllabus.
3. To develop the study skills and communication skills in formal and informal situations.

4.3 OBJECTIVES FOR LSRW

4.3.1 Listening Skills

The objectives of the Listening Skills as mentioned are,

1. To enable students to develop their listening skill so that they may appreciate its role in the LSRW skills approach to language and improve their pronunciation.

2. To equip students with necessary training in listening so that they can understand the speech of people of different backgrounds and regions.

The manual mentions the methodology to be practiced in broad terms as, "Students should be given practice in listening to the sounds of the language to be able to recognize them, to distinguish between them, to mark stress and recognize and use the right intonation in sentences" (Manual 22).

The micro skills aimed at are:

- • Listening for general content
- • Listening to fill up information
- • Intensive listening
- • Listening for specific information

4.3.2 Speaking Skills

The objectives of the speaking skills as mentioned are,

1. To make students aware of the role of speaking in English and its contribution to their success.
2. To enable students to express themselves fluently and appropriately in social and professional contexts.

The tools used to achieve these objectives are:

- Oral practice
- Role play – Individual/Group activities, (Using exercises from all the nine units of the prescribed text: *Learning English: A Communicative Approach*.)
- Just A Minute(JAM) Sessions

4.3.3 Reading Skills

The general objectives mentioned for the Reading skill are:

1. To develop an awareness in the students about the significance of silent reading and comprehension.
2. To develop the ability of students to guess the meanings of words from

context and grasp the overall message of the text, draw inferences etc.

The micro skills identified to achieve the above objectives are:

- Skimming the text
- Understanding the gist of an argument
- Identifying the topic sentence
- Inferring lexical and contextual meaning
- Understanding discourse features
- Recognizing coherence/sequencing of sentences

The manual reiterates the point that the texts meant for detailed and non-detailed study are to be used initially, and then the teacher should move on to unseen passages from authentic material such as newspaper articles, magazines etc. It is further noted that the students will be trained in reading skills using the prescribed text for detailed study. They will be examined in reading and answering questions using 'unseen' passages which may be taken from the non-detailed text or other authentic texts, such as magazines/ newspaper articles.

4.3.4 Writing Skills

The objectives of the writing skills are as follows:

1. To develop an awareness in the students about writing as an exact and formal skill.
2. To equip them with the components of different forms of writing, beginning with the lower order ones.

The students will be trained in the following micro skills to achieve the above mentioned objectives:

- Writing sentences
- Use of appropriate vocabulary
- Paragraph writing
- Coherence and cohesiveness
- Narration / description
- Note Making
- Formal and informal letter writing
- Editing a passage

4.4 STRUCTURE OF THE DETAILED TEXT *ENJOYING EVERYDAY ENGLISH*

The text for detailed study titled *Enjoying Everyday English* claims to be "a complete, stand-alone English course book that offers learners practice in reading, writing, listening, speaking, grammar and vocabulary." The course writers claim to have prepared the material keeping in view the communicative needs as well as the interests of the present-day students. They assert that the explanations, examples and exercises in the book are intended to enable learners "to use the language fluently and accurately" (Back cover).

The text comprises of six lessons. Each lesson introduces an interesting topic. The lessons are based on travel, biography, human interest, disaster management, humour and films. The text is followed by exercises to be worked out. None of the topics in the exercise part are repeated. The following shows the pattern followed by the editors in the organization of the text and exercise material.

Unit –I TRAVEL

"Heaven's Gate" by Pico Iyer

Reading	Heaven's Gate
Writing	Paragraph and descriptions
Listening	Listening for sounds
Speaking	Greeting, taking leave and introducing
Grammar	Naming words
Vocabulary	Homonyms, homophones, homographs, synonyms and antonyms

Unit –II BIOGRAPHY

"Sir CV Raman: A Path breaker in the Saga of Indian Science" by Shubashree Desikan.

Reading	Sir C.V. Raman
Writing	Work-related correspondence
Listening	Listening for words
Speaking	Making requests
Grammar	Making naming words specific(Part I)
Vocabulary	Word formation

Unit –III HUMAN INTEREST

"The Connoisseur" by Nergis Dalal

Reading	The Connoisseur
Writing	Summarising
Listening	Listening for words
Speaking	Apologising and inviting
Grammar	Making naming words specific (Part 2)
Vocabulary	Collocations

Unit –IV DISASTER MANAGEMENT

"The Cuddalore Experience" by Anu George

Reading	The Cuddalore Experience
Writing	Official reports
Listening	Listening for theme
Speaking	Congratulating, offering sympathy and condolences and making complaints
Grammar	Tenses
Vocabulary	Phrasal Verbs

Unit –V HUMOUR

"Bubbling Well Road"by Rudyard Kipling

Reading	Bubbling Well Road
Writing	Note making
Listening	Listening for details and taking notes
Speaking	Interview skills
Grammar	Adverbials and model verbs
Vocabulary	Idioms

Unit –VI FILMS

"Odds Against Us" by Satyajit Ray.

Reading	The Odds against Us
Writing	Information Transfer
Listening	Listening to announcements and directions
Speaking	Making presentations
Grammar	Conjunctions and prepositions
Vocabulary	Technical vocabulary

4.4.1. Additional Units

In addition to the six Units of the detailed text, the manual prescribes two more units, that is VII and VIII, focusing on LSRW skills, grammar and vocabulary.

Unit – VII

Exercises in the following areas

- Reading and Writing Skills
- Reading Comprehension
- Situational dialogues
- Letter writing
- Essay writing

Unit – VIII

This unit has Practice Exercises on Remedial Grammar covering,

- Common errors in English, Subject-Verb agreement, Use of Articles and Prepositions,
- Tense and aspect
- Vocabulary development covering
- Synonyms & Antonyms, one-word substitutes, prefixes & suffixes, Idioms & phrases, words often confused.

The text is followed by the exercise material. However the manual makes it clear that additional exercise material should also be used for classroom tasks. Photographs are used to produce a visual impact.

4.4.2 The book is accompanied by an audio CD. The track list has ten units. They are as follows:

Track 1 Unit 1	Listening
Track 2 Unit 2	Speaking
Track 3 Unit 2	Listening (Listening for words)
Track 4 Unit 2	Speaking (Making requests)
Track 5 Unit 3	Listening (Listening for word stress)
Track 6 Unit 3	Speaking (Making and accepting an apology, Inviting and accepting/declining an invitation)
Track 6 Unit 4	Listening
Track 7 Unit 4	Speaking (Congratulating, expressing sympathy and offering condolences, making complaints)
Track 8 Unit 5	Listening (Listening for details)
Track 9 Unit 5	Speaking (Interview skills)
Track 10 Unit 6	Listening (Listening to announcements and directions)

4.5 NON-DETAILED TEXT *INSPIRING SPEECHES AND LIVES*

Inspiring Speeches and Lives comprises of speeches by eminent personalities like John F. Kennedy, Martin Luther King, Barrack Hussein Obama and Swami Vivekananda; and biographies of Hargobind Khorana, Amartya Kumar Sen, Sam Pitroda and Mother Teresa. The editors say, "The selections in the book have the potential to impact upon the young minds and heart of the students…given the inspirational tenor and quality of the selections."

The language exercises at the end of each selection consist of glossary, comprehension, passages, paragraph expansion, précis, speech writing, word accent and other activities relating to speaking, writing and skills of group discussion. The text is arranged as follows:

SPEECHES

"Ask Not What Your Country can do for You" by John F Kennedy

"I Have a Dream" by Martin Luther King

LIVES

- Haragobind Khorana
- Dr. Amartya Kumar Sen
- Sam Pitroda
- Mother Teresa

(An example for the organization of the text and exercise material is provided in Appendix-I)

Inspiring Speeches and Lives is accompanied by a video CD. The CD shows the four speeches being delivered. The editors feel that the students will benefit immensely from these speeches by keen listening and close observation. They say, "They can learn valuable communication skills from these speeches. Aspects relating to appropriate body language postures, eye contact, gestures, pronunciation, intonation and rhythm can be studied and emulated by the students. The teachers/resource persons/trainers can use the CD speeches in many pedagogically creative ways, thus enabling the students to gain valuable insight and imbibe vital strategies of public speaking." (Editors' note)

4.6 ENGLISH LANGUAGE COMMUNICATION SKILLS LAB

Communication Skills lab is an important component in the syllabus. The students being techno savvy would find it easy to use them. The Language Lab focuses on the production and practice of sounds of language and familiarizes the students with the use of English in everyday situations and contexts.

4.6.1 Objectives

The objectives mentioned are as follows:

1. To expose the students to a variety of self-instructional, learner-friendly modes of language learning.
2. To help the students cultivate the habit of reading passages from the computer monitor, thus providing them with the required facility to face computer-based competitive exams such GRE, TOEFL, GMAT etc.,
3. To enable them to learn better pronunciation through stress on word accent, intonation, and rhythm.
4. To train them to use language effectively to face interviews, group discussions, public speaking.
5. To initiate them into greater use of the computer in resume preparation, report writing, format-making etc. (manual-7)

4.6.2 SYLLABUS

The following course content and skills are prescribed for the English Language Laboratory sessions:

1. Introduction to the Sounds of English- Vowels, Diphthongs and
2. Consonants - Introduction to Stress and Intonation
3. Situational Dialogues / Role Play.
4. Oral Presentations- Prepared and Extempore.
5. Just A Minute' Sessions (JAM).
6. Describing Objects / Situations / People
7. Information Transfer
8. Debate
9. Telephoning Skills
10. Giving Directions.

Appendix - I provides the list of books and suggested software by JNTU

4.7 III/IV YEAR B.TECH ADVANCED ENGLISH COMMUNICATION SKILLS LAB.

A student pursuing Engineering course in JNTU has the facility to use communication skills lab for learning English language in the I semester and also in III/IV semisters.

The main aim of ELCS / AECS labs is to improve Communication Skills in formal and informal situations. It is also to impart training to students through the syllabus in the theoretical aspects and practical components.

4.7.1 Introduction

English enhances the employability of students. Any employer looks for a high-degree of proficiency in English Language. It is the language of opportunities. The introduction of language lab teaching/learning plays a crucial role at this stage. It enables the students to expedite the process of improving learning skills, with more emphasis on LSRW (Listening, Speaking, and Reading& Writing). Recognizing the needs of the students, the manual says:

> The introduction of English Language Lab is considered essential at third year level. At this stage, the students need to prepare themselves for their careers which may require them to listen to, read, speak and write in English both for their professional and interpersonal communication in the globalized context. (112)

These labs train the students in Language Skills, Soft Skills, Inter Personal Skills, Decision Making, Business Communication, Pre-Placement Training, Corporate Readiness, GRE etc.

4.7.2 Objectives:

The lab focuses on using computer-aided multimedia instruction for language development. The framers have specified the objectives as follows:

To improve the student's fluency in English, through a well developed vocabulary and enable them to listen to English spoken at normal conversation speed by educated English speakers and respond appropriately in different socio-cultural and professional contexts.

4.7.3 Syllabus:

The following course content is prescribed for the AECSL students:

Functional English:
Starting a conversation – responding appropriately and relevantly – using the right body language – role play in different situation.

Vocabulary Building:
Synonyms, antonyms – word roots – one word substitutes – prefixes, suffixes and study of origin – analogy – idioms and phrases.

Group Discussion:
Dynamics of Group Discussion – Intervention, summarizing, modulation of voice – body language – relevance – fluency and coherence.

Interview Skills:
Concept and process – Pre-interview planning, opening strategies – Interview through tele and video conferencing.

Resume Writing:
Structure and presentation-planning defining the career objective – projecting ones strengths and skill sets summary - formats and styles - letter writing.

Reading Comprehension:
Reading for facts, guessing meanings from context, scanning, skimming, inferring meaning critical reading.

Technical Report Writing:
Exposure and training in types of formats and styles, subject matter - organization, clarity, coherence and style, planning, data-collection, tools, analysis are prescribed.

4.7.4 The following books are to be kept in the laboratory library

1. *Spoken English* (CIEFL) in 3 volumes with 6 cassettes, OUP.
2. *English Pronouncing Dictionary* by Daniel Jones Current Edition with CD, Cambridge UP.
3. *Spoken English* by R.K. Bansal and J.B. Harrison, 2006 Edn. Orient Longman.
4. *English Language Communication: A Reader cum Lab Manual* by A Ramakrishna Rao, Dr. Natanam & Prof. S.A.. Sankaranarayanan, Anuradha Publications, Chennai.
5. *Speaking English Effectively* by Krishna Mohan & NP Singh. Macmillan.
6. *A Practical Course in English Pronunciation,* (with two Audio cassettes)

by J. Sethi, Kamalesh Sadanand and D.V. Jindal, Prentice Hall of India Pvt Ltd., New Delhi.

7. *A Textbook of English Phonetics for Indian Students* by T. Balasubramanian, Macmillan.

8. *English Skills for Technical Students* by WBSCTE with British Council, Orient Longman.

Books Suggested for English Language Lab Library are to be located within the lab in addition to the CDs of the books which are loaded on the system.

4.7.5 Minimum Requirement for ELCS and AECS Lab:

The requirements of the lab as mentioned in the *Manual* are that the lab must have a platform of good configuration, computers with Advanced Remote Monitoring facility, which enables the teacher to monitor all the students through a master console.

The English Language Lab shall have two parts.

1. The Computer aided Language Lab for 60 students with 60 systems, one master console, LAN facility and English language software for self- study by learners

2. The Communication Skills Lab with movable chairs and audio-visual aids with a P4 System, a T.V., a digital stereo –audio & video system and camcorder etc.

System Requirement (Hardware component)
Computer network with Lan with minimum 60 multimedia systems with the following specifications:

1. P – IV Processor
2. Speed – 2.8 GHZ
3. RAM – 512 MB Minimum
4. Hard Disk – 80 GB
5. Headphones of High quality

Books Suggested for English Language Lab Library are to be located within the lab in addition to the CDs of the text book which are loaded on the systems. See Appendix-I for suggested software and recommended books for ELCS and AECS Laboratories.

SECTION B
I Year B.Tech English Syllabus for Kakatiya University.

4.8 INTRODUCTION

According to the preface of the text *Communicative English for Engineers and Professionals,* the syllabus has been designed to meet the global demand of students of Science, Technology and Computer Education. It is a combination of two media: Written Communication and Oral Communication. In written communication an attempt is made to help the professionals to improve their written communicative abilities. In oral communication various aspects have been covered to improve the spoken English of young professionals. It gives a conceptual framework to teachers teaching in Engineering Colleges. The book entitled *Communicative English for Engineers and Professionals* is edited by Dr. M. Surendra Kumar and Prof. G. Damodar. An essay "The American Scholar" from *Selected Essays* by Emerson, Ralph Waldo is for general reading purpose.

The syllabus objectives are not mentioned in the book and no instruction booklet/manual is supplied for teachers and students.

4.8.1 Syllabus

Communicative English for Engineers and Professionals is entirely devoted to grammar and certain topics in communicative skills. The following are the contents:

1. Grammar and Vocabulary

  i.   The Sentence

  ii. Simple, Compound, Complex and Compound Complex Sentences

  iii. Transformation of Sentences (word order)

  iv. Transformation of Sentences (clause order)

  v.   Direct and Indirect Speech

  vi. Articles

  vii. Verb

  viii. Phrasal Verbs

  ix. Tense

  x.   Prepositions

  xi. Conjunctions and Connectors

  xii. Words often Confused

  xiii. One word substitutes

  xiv. Concord

2. Comprehension

3. Writing Skills

  i.   Paragraph writing

  ii. Letter writing

  iii. Report writing

  iv. Dialogue writing

4. Oral communication

  i.   On pronunciation

  ii. Social Conversations

  iii. Formal Speech

  iv. Group discussion

  v.   Interview Techniques

4.8.2 Suggested Reading

The following books are recommended as suggested ʽreading.

R.C. Sharma and Krishna Mohan, *Business Correspondence & Report Writing*.

1. Thomson and Martinet, *A Practical English Grammar English Usage & Detection of Errors*.
2. Grand Taylor, *Conversational English*.
3. David Green, *English Grammar Composition Structures*.
4. ML Tickoo and Subramaniyam, *Intermediate English Grammar Usage and Composition*.
5. Thorat, *Enriching English, UG Level*
6. G. Damodar, *Listening & Speaking Skills*.

Syllabus and the materials play an imperative role in the design of any language programme. The materials should be of student's interest and the teaching methodology creative otherwise they lose their motivation. Selection of appropriate teaching materials is the most important feature in practice. In fact, a language teacher or institution should provide teaching materials that will fit the specific subject areas of particular learners according to their needs for academic purposes. "Materials provide a stimulus to learning. Good materials do not teach: they encourage learners to learn" (Hutchinson and Waters 107).

4.8.3 Conclusion

This chapter presents the Syllabus being followed currently in the Engineering Colleges which come under the jurisdiction of JNTU and KU. It is apparent that JNTU syllabus incorporates the elements of macro skills, grammar, and vocabulary whereas for KU syllabus, the basic strands are grammar and vocabulary.

C H A P T E R 5

Critical Analysis of Current Syllabi

5.1 INTRODUCTION

English has become the predominant language for communication in the world today. Indian engineering graduates have required technical skills but lack in communication skills. A large number of professionals have to now travel to many continents. Hence English is the need of the hour in Indian class rooms and English Language Teaching plays a key role in engineering students' employability. In this context the syllabus material/textbook and methods used are crucial.

ELT materials (textbooks) play a very significant role in language classrooms for a number of pedagogical, ideological and practical reasons and there has been a lot of debate in recent years on the actual role of materials in teaching English as a Second Language. Though there are arguments on both the potential and the limitations of materials, the syllabus and the material add pedagogical value towards a language program. Other aspects that have been debated in recent years include textbook design and practicality, suitability to a particular group, methodological validity, the role and novelty of textbooks, the authenticity of materials in terms of their representation of language and cultural components.

English language teaching has many substantial components but the indispensable constituent to many ELT classrooms and programs are the textbooks and instruction materials used by language instructors. According to Hutchinson and Torres, "The textbook is an almost universal element of English language teaching. Millions of copies are sold every year, and numerous aid projects have been set up to produce them in [various] countries...No teaching-learning situation, it seems, is complete until it has its relevant textbook" (315). They pointed out that textbooks play a pivotal role in innovation. They reveal assumptions and tenets about the nature of language teaching and learning, and reflect aims and standards that are to be reached in the classroom. They also provide a sense of "security "and "accountability" to the teacher/learner. As they further observe,

> Education is a complex and messy matter. What the textbook does is to create a certain degree of order within potential chaos. It is a visible and workable framework around which the many forces and demands of the teaching-learning process can cohere to provide the basis

of security and accountability that is necessary for purposeful action in the classroom. (Hutchinson and Torres 327)

Sheldon expresses has the same opinion with this observation and suggests that textbooks not only "... represent the visible heart of any ELT program but also offer considerable advantages for both the student and the teacher when the books are being used in the classroom. Students often harbour expectations about using a textbook in their particular language classroom program and believe that published materials have more credibility than teacher-generated or 'in-house' materials" (237).

Haycroft suggests that one of the main advantages of using textbooks is that they are psychologically needed for students since their improvement and achievement can be measured concretely when we use them.

Neill has indicated that textbooks are generally sensitive to students' requirements, though they are not designed exclusively for them, they are useful in terms of time and money, and they can and should allow for adaptation and improvisation. He further adds, the textbooks yield an adequate return on investment, are relatively economical and engage low lesson preparation time, where teacher-generated materials can be time consuming, costly and also defective quality wise. Therefore textbooks can decrease "possible occupational burden" and allow teachers the chance to spend their time undertaking more meaningful pursuits.

Cunningsworth emphasizes the usefulness of the text books, which have the potential of playing several supplementary roles in the English curriculum. They are a valuable resource for self-directed learning, for presentation of ideas and actions, and a reference source for students. In a curriculum, they reflect pre-determined learning objectives and support for fresh graduate teachers who have yet to gain confidence in teaching. Though some theorists have alluded to the inherent danger of the inexperienced teacher who may make use of a textbook as a pedagogic support, such an overreliance may actually have the opposite consequence of saving students from a teacher's inefficiency.

Sheldon's opinion is that the eventual ground for dissatisfaction and skepticism with many ELT textbooks is that they are often considered as the "...tainted end-product of an author's or a publisher's desire for quick profit" (239). He further says that too many textbooks are often marketed with grand artificial claims by their authors and publishers, yet these same books tend to contain serious theoretical problems, design flaws, and practical shortcomings. They also "...present disjointed material that is either too limited or too generalized in a superficial and flashy manner and the vast array of single edition, now defunct [text] books produced during the past ten years testifies to the market consequences of teachers' verdicts on such practices" (239).

Thus the arguments for using a textbook are:

- A textbook is a framework which regulates and times the programs.
- In the eyes of learners, no textbook means no purpose.
- Without a textbook, learners think their learning is not taken seriously.
- In many situations, a textbook can serve as a syllabus.
- A textbook provides ready-made teaching texts and learning tasks.
- A textbook is a cheap way of providing learning materials.
- A learner without a textbook is out of focus and teacher-dependent.
- Perhaps most important of all, for novice teachers a textbook means security, guidance, and support.(Ur.183-195)

The counter-arguments are:

- If every group of students has different needs, no one textbook can be a response to all differing needs.
- Topics in a textbook may not be relevant for and interesting to all.
- A textbook is confining, i.e., it inhibits teachers' creativity.
- A textbook of necessity sets prearranged sequence and structure that may not be realistic and situation-friendly.
- Textbooks have their own rationale, and as such it cannot by their nature to cater for a variety of levels, learning styles, and learning strategies that often exist in the class.
- Most important of all, perhaps teachers may find themselves as mediators with no free hand and a slave, in fact, to others' judgments about what is good and what is not (Ur 183-195).

The textbooks may be too inflexible to be used as instructional material or they may justly help teaching and learning processes. However, there can be no denying the fact that textbooks still hold enormous status. There has been a movement since the 1970's to make learners the center of language instruction and it is certainly appropriate to view textbooks as resources in attaining aims and objectives which have already been set in terms of learner needs.

5.2 NEED FOR TEXTBOOK EVALUATION

As Brown says, the textbooks should not necessarily determine the aims themselves (components of teaching and learning) or become the aims but they should always be in the service of the teachers and learners. Consequently, one must make every effort to establish and apply a wide variety of relevant and contextually appropriate criteria for the evaluation of the textbooks that are used in the language classrooms. Cunningsworth says that one should also ensure "that careful selection is made, and that the materials selected closely reflect [the needs of the learners and] the aims, methods, and values of the teaching program" (7).

Sheldon has offered several other reasons for textbook evaluation. He recommends that the selection of an ELT textbook often indicates a significant administrative and didactic decision in which there is considerable professional, financial, or even political investment.

A meticulous evaluation, therefore, would enable the material producers to distinguish between the available textbooks in the market. Furthermore, it would provide a sense of awareness with a book's content, thus assisting educators in identifying the particular strengths and weaknesses in textbooks already in use. It leads ultimately in assisting teachers with making optimum use of a book's strong points and recognizing the shortcomings of certain exercises, tasks, and entire texts. The advantage of textbook evaluation is required because it is helpful in teacher advancement and professional development. As Cunningsworth and Ellis suggest:

> Evaluation of textbooks make teachers intuit beyond impressionistic assessments and it helps them to attain useful, accurate, systematic, and appropriate insights into the overall nature of textbook material. Therefore textbook evaluation is potentially a valuable means to carry out action research as well as a form of professional empowerment and improvement. In the same way, it can also be an important element of teacher training programs for it serves the dual purpose of helping student teachers become aware of significant features in textbooks while also familiarizing them with a wide range of published language instruction materials. (38)

The untrained teachers with heavy workload try to complete the syllabus ignoring its aims and objectives. According to Williams, "it is ironical that those teachers who rely most heavily on the textbooks are the ones least qualified to interpret its intentions or evaluate its content and method" (251).

It has to be noted that a textbook plays a crucial role in the Indian ELT classrooms. Right from the beginners to the advanced learners a textbook, for various reasons mentioned above, has become a necessity.

This chapter is divided into Section A and Section B. Section A gives a critical analysis of English Syllabus offered in Engineering colleges of JNTU, Hyderabad and Section B of Kakatiya University English syllabus for Engineering students.

The critical analysis of JNTU and Kakatiya University are examined by applying a set of universal parameters.

SECTION A

5.3 INTRODUCTION

JNTU Hyderabad has about 200 Engineering colleges both the government and private managed put together. The teaching staff is recruited by the respective institutions mostly. The eligibility criteria being post graduation, fresh postgraduates enter as teachers without undergoing any training.

5.4 THE TEXTBOOKS AND THE MATERIAL

JNTU Hyderabad prescribed two textbooks along with CDs. The detailed text, *Enjoying Every Day English* is edited by A Rama Krisna Rao and the non-detailed text *Inspiring Speeches and Lives* is edited by Yadava Raju, B.and C. Murali Krishna. An instruction manual is supplied for teachers and students which states the guidelines and objectives of prescribed course. The books follow "PPP" (presentation, practice, production) pattern which is suitable for Indian classrooms.

The detailed text *Enjoying Every Day English* presents selections chosen with the learner's interests in mind. The text along with its vocabulary and exercises aims to prepare the students in using the language accurately and fluently. To achieve this goal the designers have presented frequent vocabulary, important concepts in grammar and syntax and the four skills LSRW with exercises. The students work through real unedited selections (of course with assistance from the teacher) of the detailed text and move on to engineered reading selections of the non-detailed text (here they are expected to read on their own). There is a good deal of supporting explanatory and exercise material.

The text for non-detailed study *Inspiring Speeches and Lives* is for extensive reading/reading for pleasure by the students. Hence, it is suggested that they read it on their own with topics selected for discussion in the class. The time should be utilized for working out the exercises given after each section, as also for supplementing the exercises with authentic materials of a similar kind for example, from newspaper articles, advertisements, promotional material etc. However, the stress in this syllabus is on skill development and practice of language skills.

In addition to the students being exposed to the narrative selections and exercises, the texts also provide practice in the use of the two important areas in text materials. They are firstly, the use of the physical features such as the table of contents, glossaries and reference lists. Secondly, it is to read and interpret the visual features embedded in the text like tables, charts, diagrams, graphs, line drawings and illustrations.

Both the texts mirror the advancements in material production, and definitely help the teacher/learner in the teaching/learning process.

5.5 LAYOUT, DESIGN AND PRICE OF THE TEXT

The size of the text book is A4 and the quality of the paper is durable. The titles *Enjoying Every Day English* and *Inspiring Speeches and Lives* do attract the learner. The quality of the detailed text book paper is durable and the font of the text is clear. The colour scheme, the highlighted areas and the presentation of information in a simple format makes one understand easily and follow the text. Photographs, pictures, tables, graphs and charts are used where required which are for student's comprehension (see Appendix: I).

The size of the non-detailed text is smaller than the detailed text and the quality of the paper is low. However standard quality of editing and publishing is maintained for both the books. The price of the detailed textbook is one hundred and seventy five and for non-detailed text the price is one hundred and ten rupees (See Appendix: I). The price though on the higher side is inevitable as they carry CDs: an audio CD for the detailed and video CD for the non-detailed texts.

5.6 TIME FRAME FOR THE B.TECH ENGLISH PROGRAMME

JNTU, Hyderabad B.Tech course offers English as theory in the classroom and as practicals in the Language Laboratory (ELCS–English Language Communication Skills Lab) for the first academic year. I-B.Tech is for one academic year. Generally the instruction for class work runs from October to April. Approximately 80 hours are allocated for classroom teaching and another 80 hours for laboratory.

Advanced English Communication Skills Lab (AECS) is introduced either in III or IV year of the B.Tech programme for one semester. Approximately 40 hours are allocated (i.e. only for one semester).

5.7 STRENGTH AND STANDARD OF THE STUDENTS

Indian class rooms are overcrowded with a large number of students and with least facilities. Universities permit an intake of 60 to 65 for each class. The same is the case with JNTU, Hyderabad. However the number may be go up to 100 in some colleges. The students are from rural and urban areas who studied in the regional media or English medium.

The students entering the programme have already been exposed to years of classroom practice of English language. They have been exposed at one time or other (and with greater or lesser amounts of success) to the basics of the language and have a fair amount of vocabulary. Their conversational levels are low and make many mistakes in grammar, lexicon and pronunciation. They understand more difficult language than they can produce. So far they have been exposed to strictly controlled material.

However to be more practical, the students from Telugu medium and other regional media are not well equipped with the required basics as a consequence of various factors in their previous study. This situation is a pedagogic challenge in the teaching and learning processes.

5.8 HETEROGENEITY OF THE CLASS

People who have the same interests or objectives are defined as a group who organize themselves to work or act together. Since the learners in the engineering colleges have common goals and objectives, the class is considered as a group. The group is heterogeneous as the students have a range of earlier academic achievement and varying levels of oral and written proficiency in the language of instruction. The reasons for heterogeneity in Indian class rooms are i) learners are from various regions, religions, castes, classes and languages. ii) the medium of instruction, the flexibility in selecting the first and second language at school level and also introducing English subject in higher classes. Because of these reasons learners in Engineering colleges are found with different levels of linguistic and communicative competence.

5.9 THE DETAILED TEXT

The text *Enjoying Every Day English* is for detailed study, the accompanying audio CD has listening and speaking materials related to the corresponding sections in the book. The selections are of universal appeal. All the other sections of the lesson are tightly connected with the narrative selection either as a preparation for it or as an extension of it.

5.9.1 Stating the plan of the text

An instruction booklet is supplied along with the text books which state the purpose and the objectives of the syllabus for the total course. The booklet is informative and quite comprehensive regarding the information it gives. It deals with the entire academic plan of the programme. The rules in force, the syllabus of the various courses, the time schedule, the number of periods allotted to each course and the assessment process are presented. It is a useful guide for the teachers and learners.

5.9.2 Objectives of the syllabus

The objectives of the English course broadly stated are three in number. The first is to improve the language proficiency of the students in English with emphasis on LSRW (Listening, Speaking, Reading, Writing) skills. The second is to equip the students to study academic subjects with greater facility through the theoretical and practical components of the English syllabus. The third objective is more attuned to the needs of the graduate learners. It is to develop the study skills and communication skills in formal and informal situations.

The objectives are suitable to the needs of the students. In addition to the above broad objectives, the manual also gives a list of particular elements (sub skills) to be emphasized in the teaching process. However one has to admit that the setting of objectives is a bit vague as only the broader areas are mentioned.

5.9.3 Content and Language Type

The textbook contains the lessons that are the extracts of various topics: Travel, Biography, Human Interest, Disaster Management, Humour and Films which are of general interest for graduate level students. The language is within the range of Engineering students. The criteria deemed to be important include whether or not the language is at the right level or of the right type for the students and whether the progression of new language is both logical and appropriate for students. The language included in the materials is realistic and authentic. The textbook encourages socio-cultural and local language. This is due to the students' requirement to use the language they had learnt to engage in purposeful and genuine situations or to talk about themselves and their lives in a meaningful manner. In general one would expect there to be some intelligible connection or sequence between what students have previously learned and what they are learning now. In this aspect the contents are realistically designed by taking into consideration the learner's previous learning. The book places a fair bit of emphasis on grammatical structures, functions and accuracy.

With respect to vocabulary, the text makes an effort to sensitize learners to the structure of the lexicon of English and to the various relationships that exist within it. Most 'productive' or 'active' lexis and identifiable fixed phrases, for instance, are presented in the controlled practice activities while some 'receptive' or 'passive' lexis is introduced through reading and listening tasks during which the students are required to decipher meaning from the surrounding context. In addition, a few useful vocabulary building exercises are included.

5.9.4 Organisation of the material

A quick glance through the table of contents gives the idea of what the text contains and how it would be useful for the students. (See appendix: I)

The textbook lessons and linguistic items are organized from simple to complex level but which may not cater to the specific requirements of a heterogeneous group. Uniform sequence is followed in organising exercises from unit one to six. The exercises are presented with title instruction, illustrations and the use of tables with different colours and shades.

The content of the text has been divided into six units. Each Unit is an extract from the areas like: Travel, Biography, Human Interest, Disaster Management, Humor, Films. These units are expected to form the basis for teaching of the following skills:

- Reading
- Writing
- Listening
- Speaking
- Grammar
- Vocabulary

5.9.5 Reading Skills

Reading is not just recognizing the sound of a printed word. It stimulates and activates the thinking faculty of the reader, and as a result, grants him the power of judgment. Reading is for i)Meaning Factual recall, Finding the main idea,

Understanding new vocabulary from context, Confirmation of content, Determining cause and effect, Distinguishing fact from opinion, Drawing conclusion ii) Reference iii) Syntax iv) Prediction.

The learner embroils himself to achieve the challenging task of comprehension, which primarily begins with decoding the words, and proceeds to analyze the integrity or coherence among the sentences and ends up with bringing out the hidden or implied meaning. According to Gough: "Reading is a linear, almost mechanical process that starts with processing each letter, combining letters into words, looking up the meaning of these words in lexical memory, storing meaning briefly in short memory and finally combining word meanings to form first sentence meaning and then meanings for the larger portion of the text." (page number N.A.)

All the six Units of the text book have lessons for reading. Each lesson is followed by exercises on reading skills. The exercises are organized in the following manner:

1. The first exercise is 'word study' which aims to introduce and draw attention of the learner to new words. The exercise is to match the words with their definitions. The words are taken from the lesson to guess the meaning from the context.

2. The next exercises are on 'reading comprehension' which are to make the learner to comprehend the text. The exercise has statements which are followed by three options to choose the best ending. A second type of exercise for testing the comprehension of the student is questions with short answers (based on the text) are asked.

The following exercises are from I Unit Lesson "Heaven's Gate," from the page number 1 to 6. Each exercise with its title instruction and few bits from the exercises are given as an example.

a. Word study

Match the words below with their definitions. Try to guess the meanings from the context. After you have finished, use a dictionary to check your answers.

a. Impromptu	The biggest or longest street that goes
b. Pristine	Through a town.
c. Forage	Stylish and fashionable.
d. Chic	Fresh, in very good condition.
e. drag	To go from place to place searching,
	Especially for food.
	Done or said without earlier planning
	or
	Preparation.

b. Reading Comprehension:

Choose the best ending to each of these sentences.

a. The author's account of Ladakh is based on:

II.	his reading
III.	his visit to the place
IV.	what others have told him

b. At 15,000 feet, Leh:

I.	looks like a vast snow-covered field.
II.	Has houses built close to one another.
III.	Is completely uninhabited

2. Write brief answers to these questions.

a. What animals and trees did the writer find in the Nubra Valley?

b. What do you think the writer means when he says, 'I saw faces that spoke of Lhasa Hearat, even Samarkand.

5.9.6 Writing Skills

The productive skill writing is as important as speaking skill for an engineering student. He needs to prepare notes and write exams during the study, and after the study at work place most of his time is spent writing to communicate and in documentation.

All the six units are followed by exercises in writings skills. The sequence of the exercises on writing skills are: paragraphs and descriptions, work related correspondence- official letters, Email, memorandum, official reports, and information transfer.

The following exercises are from the first lesson "Heaven's Gate," from pages 7 to 10. Only a few bits from the exercises are given here as example.

Paragraph Writing

To communicate clearly when one writes, one needs to organize writing in the form of paragraphs. A paragraph is a small set of carefully arranged sentences on a topic. Here are some guidelines to help you write paragraphs. Think about the topic on which you want to write a paragraph and list the ideas that come to your mind.

- State the main idea of the paragraph in a sentence, which will be its topic sentence.
- Arrange the sentences in a chronological or logical order.
- Use complete sentences of different lengths and structures.
- _______________
- _______________

Read the sample paragraph below and find the topic sentence as well as the connectives and reference words that make it coherent. Note how the main idea is developed with the help of details and examples. Do you think one of the words in the topic sentence could be the title of the paragraph?

Euthanasia is the act of helping a person who is terminally ill die painlessly. It is considered as an option only when the patient is either in terrible pain and longs for release or is in a prolonged comatose state Euthanasia can be achieved by administering drugs that lead to a painless death. It could, on the other hand, simply involve taking the patient off all life-support systems—which some doctors may do more readily than killing the patient with the help of a lethal drug. The act is an offence in most countries and has been made legal only in places like Holland and Belgium. The two sides of the controversy regarding euthanasia involve the questions of the right of an individual to die with dignity under a well-defined set of circumstances and that of the essential sacredness of life.

5.9.7 Listening skills

Listening is not simply a transfer of information. The fundamental information processing paradigm sees it as a perfect encoding-decoding process. Cognitive science looks at listening as a construction process. According to relevance theory understanding is both decoding and inferential process. The listener may appear to be inactive while listening, but he is constantly engaged in the construction of a message. If the students do not learn to listen effectively, they will be unable to take part in oral communication. If he fails to understand the message due to various reasons, it is referred to as communication breakdown. This means that the listener has not paid attention to the message or he has not understood it. Hence the students should be trained to listen. They have to pay attention to what they hear, process, understand, interpret and evaluate in order to respond. They have to listen to in real life, classrooms and in interactions.

The exercises on listening skills are organized as: listening to sounds, listening for words, listening for word stress, listening for theme, listening for details and notes, listening to announcements and directions.

The following exercises are from the Unit "Heaven's Gate." Only a few bits from the exercises are given from the pages 12 to 13.

A. Listening skills

Listening for sounds involves focusing your attention on the sounds that make up words and recognizing them when they appear in other words. This is the first step towards leaning the sounds of a language and distinguishing one word from another.

1. Listen to the numbered sets of words played to you. For every set of words you hear on the CD, there is a corresponding set of printed words. Underline the letter or letters that represent the same sound in each set. (For example, the underlined letters in 'ma<u>t</u>' and '<u>t</u>op' stand for the same sound.)

   a. (i) white   (ii) height
      (iii) sky   (iv) lie
   b. (i) laughter (ii) phantom
      (iii) five   (iv) cough
   c. (i) water   (ii) squeeze
      (iii) one   (iv) switch
   d. (i) jam   (ii) gentle
      (iii) bridge (iv) soldier
   e. (i) air   (ii) there
      (iii) wear   (iv) scarce

2. Listen to the numbered words played to you, for each word you hear on the CD, there is a corresponding printed word. Label it 1 and 2 depending on whether it ends with a /s/ sound or a /z/ sound. Request the teacher to play the CD again if you need to listen to the sound more than once. (Few words are taken from the text book)

   a. chiefs
   b. doors
   c. boxes
   d. months
   e. dreams

These exercises provide ear training to listen to the sounds accurately.

The students are given instruction on active listening. With the help of the CD that accompanies the text, the students practice exercises of listening and identifying sounds.

5.9.8 Speaking Skills

Oral language is important for effective communication and social development. Effective speaking is an essential component of success whether it is at the interpersonal, inter- group, intra-groups or organizational levels.

Effective speaking centers around the usage of words meaningfully and in ordered way, in the pitch, modulation and tone adopted. Problems in using language are often seen in those who do not understand language. They have difficulty with the spoken grammar or putting their ideas into words in an ordered manner. They omit words or word endings or use words in the wrong order. Another common problem seen in the students is their difficulty in recalling the words they know. They face retrieval problems. Helping to convert passive vocabulary into active is one of the ways to counter this tendency. The learners should be made aware of the grammatical features like tag questions, ellipses, co-ordination, finite clauses and contracted forms which are made use of in the spoken English. What is required here is the transference of these structures, which they have already practiced in their grammar exercises.

The Syllabus for speaking skill uses Communicative English to perform some preliminary communicative functions required in the course of everyday social and professional interactions of the students. Topics like Greeting, Introducing and taking leave, Making requests, Apologizing and inviting, Congratulating, Offering sympathy and condolences, Making complaints, Interview skills, Making presentations etc. are covered. The students being bilingual should be provided an opportunity to engage in the activities genuinely. In order to become active learners they need to talk and interact with other students and teachers. Talk that is connected to doing something, solving a problem, carrying out an experiment is often called as exploratory talk. This involves the unconscious processes of thinking aloud, speculating, formulating ideas, reasoning, justifying and evaluating the types of language that one needs to be able to communicate their understanding. Consciously they learn to probe, recast, explain and discuss. The activities completed in the first year should lead to the latter processes in the advanced course. Non-

verbal clues such as facial expressions, gestures, contextual clues to meaning also are essential.

The following exercises from the lesson "Heaven's Gate," is given as an example from pages 13 to 16.

A. Greeting, Taking Leave and Introducing

Read and listen to the dialogues below. You will find people greeting and taking leave of one another and introducing themselves or others. Note the language used to perform these functions.

(Mrs. Shined and Mr. Patil meet at the bank. They take the same bus to work every day, but don't know each other very well.)

Mrs. Shinde: Good morning Mr. Patil.

Mr. Patil: Good morning. Mrs. Shinde. How are you?

Mrs. Shinde: I'm very well, thank you. And how are you. Mr. Patil.

Mr. Patil: I'm fine, thanks. I'm waiting to get my passbook updated.

Mrs. Shinde: I need to get a demand draft made. Goodbye. Mr. Patil.

Mr. Patil: Bye!

Exercises

1. Look at some expressions used to greet people and take leave of them. Read each item and repeat it for practice. Note the use of contracted form such as 'I'm for 'I am" and 'you'll' for 'you will.'

a. Good morning, how are you?
b. I'm very well, thank you. What about you?
c. I'm fine, thanks.
d. We haven't met for quite some time, have we?
e. It's a pleasure to see you
f. It was nice meeting you, but I'm afraid I have to go now.
g. I must leave. I hope you'll excuse me.
h. That's quite all right. I hope we can meet again soon.
i. Yes, we must. /Yes, I hope so too, /Yes, please do come over
j. Bye, bye!

5.9.9 Grammar

Grammar is important in language teaching, particularly when English is learnt as a second language. Without a good knowledge of grammar, language development will be severely constrained. Learning grammar should emphasize not merely structure or sentence patterns but also its meaning and use. In the case of vocabulary, grammar shows how lexical items should be combined into a good sentence so that meaningful and communicative expressions can be formed. In other words by learning grammar students can express meanings in the form of phrases, clauses and sentences. Rigorous practice is recommended to achieve this end. To summarize, grammar practice in an English classroom is directed at the acquisition of implicit knowledge of a grammatical structure. That is the sort of the knowledge which is required for applying the structure effortlessly in their communication.

To equip the students with the basic knowledge of grammar, the six Units covered: Naming words, Making naming words specific (Part-1), Making naming words specific, (Part-2), Tenses, Adverbial and modal verbs, Conjunctions and prepositions.

The following exercises from the lesson "Heaven's Gate" is given from pages 16 to 24.

A. Nouns

We use nouns to refer to animals, people, places and things.

e.g. dog, Amar, daughter, Gandhi Marg, college, key, water

B. Kinds and uses

Proper nouns:
- The specific names by which we know an individual animal, a person, a lace, such as an institution, a building or a town, or something such as a month, a day of the week, a reason or a festival.

Blackie, Salma, Jawaharlal Nehru Tehnological University, Sky view Towers, Nasik, January, Sunday, Deepavali

*Note that all proper nous begin with a capital letter.

- Common nouns: words that name people, animals, places and things of the same kind parrot (as in my parrot, Rani), doctor (as in Chander, a doctor), hospital (as in a big hospital), ribbon (as in a ribbon for my hair)

*Note that all common nouns begin with a low-case letter.

Exercise

There are errors in each of the sentences below. Correct them and rewrite the sentences.

a. The churches here are many centuries old.

b. Why don't you use a plier to hold the watch cell?

c. I am writing on behalf of the Company to requests you to attend an interview on Wednesday, 2 April in our office at techno city centre.

d. The steel bar is 30 foots long, and it weighs 250 kilograms.

e. This book has photoes of hospital equipments.

f. She is doing a course on designing aircrafts.

g. We need three breads and one butter for the sandwichs.

h. Look at the flock of bees around the hive!

vi. i.The Reddies spent a lot on their children's educations.

j. How many clothings would four peoples need?

5.9.10 Vocabulary

Thornbury says, "Without grammar very little can be conveyed, without vocabulary nothing can be conveyed" (13).

The level of difficulty of language depends on lexis (content words) not on syntax (structure). For engineering students an essential recognition vocabulary of at least 5,000-10,000 word families is needed.

Bearing in mind the crucial role credited to vocabulary learning in second or foreign language learning, one can recognize the importance given to vocabulary in teaching. Several research studies have dealt with lexical problems, namely, troubles which language learners face in vocabulary learning. The research findings have discovered that lexical problems frequently obstruct communication. As a matter of fact, communication breaks down when people do not use the accurate words (Allen).

According to Huckin and Bloch, since learners depend on vocabulary as their first resource, a rich vocabulary makes the skills of listening, speaking, reading, and writing easier to perform. Nation's view is that "there has been continuing interest in whether there is a language knowledge threshold which marks the boundary between having and not having sufficient language knowledge for successful language use" (144). Historically, experienced teachers such as West (1926) considered one unknown word in every fifty words to be the minimum threshold necessary for the adequate comprehension of a text.

Thornbury argues that most adult second language learners "will be lucky to have acquired 5,000 word families even after several years of study." Then he states that "this relatively slow progress has less to do with aptitude than with exposure." Based on his vocabulary research, he concludes that "the average classroom L2 learner will experience nothing like the quantity nor the quality of exposure that the L1 infant receives" (20). Nation states that it has been calculated that "a classroom learner would need more than eighteen years of classroom exposure to supply the same amount of vocabulary input that occurs in just one year in natural settings" (225).

In the text, the word study immediately follows the reading section, where students are asked to match the words with meanings and check in the dictionary. If learners remembered words after seeing them only once, then vocabulary exercises would not be necessary. It is every language teacher's experience that in order to make vocabulary "active" rigorous practice is necessary. All too often at the intermediate level, student's vocabularies stop growing because it is assumed that practice is appropriate only for the beginners. The vocabulary section ends the Selection. The exercises are meant to sensitize the learners to the structure of the English lexicon and to the various relationships that exist within it.

The exercises covered in JNTU text book on vocabulary are Homonyms, Homophones, Homographs, Synonyms and Antonyms, Word formation, Collocations, Phrasal verbs, Idioms, Technical vocabulary etc.

The following exercises are from the lesson "Heaven's Gate," from page numbers 24 to 30.

a. Homonyms, Homophones, Homographs

Homonyms are words that have the same spelling and pronunciation, but have different meanings. Such words, therefore look and sound alike, but are listed as separate entries in a dictionary. While reading, you will be able to understand their meanings from hints that you get from the words and sentences around them. Look at the examples of homonyms below. Some of them have more meanings than those listed here.

Bank (land along the side of a river)/*bank* (a place where you keep your money)

Drill (a machine use for making holes in something)/*drill* (repeating a lesson, exercise, etc., many times)

Exercise

Fill in the blanks in the sentence pairs with words that either sound the same or are spelt the same.

    a.   Who won the race? The .... or the tortoise?

          Tie up your .... It is falling over your eyes.

    b.   I'll be travelling for one working...................

          Pankaj feels .... after the operation.

    c.   What would my .... salary be?

          .... poisoning can be very dangerous.

Notes on Synonyms and Antonyms is given and followed by exercises. One sample example is taken from the text.

    a. diffident: confident, difficult, tolerant
    b. extempore: careful, extraordinary, well-prepared
    c. consent: forbid, resent, permit
    d. amicable: negative, surprising, unfriendly
    e. ambiguity: clarity, guilt, liveliness

5.9.11 Methodology

The syllabus is basically designed on the principles of Communicative approach. The major hurdle that an English teacher has to face is a lack of motivation amongst the students. Learner centered approach in ELT is a boon that aids the teacher to effectively overcome this obstacle. When the student is empowered and a justifiable balance maintained between guidance and freedom, the learner gets motivated to take positive steps towards language learning. The resultant experience of the language and the confidence gained thereof from individual achievement goes a long way in the overall progress of the student.

The teacher adopts a bilingual method of teaching because of Telugu medium students. As the class is heterogeneous, the teacher is expected to read the lines, explain the text and make them practice the exercises at the end of each lesson. This being a time consuming process, not much time is left for other activities. However the teacher tries to include tasks, activities and involve the students in interactive sessions.

5.10 NON-DETAILED TEXT

Non-detailed text *Inspiring Speeches and Lives* is a text comprising some select speeches and biographies, each followed by English language improvement exercises. It is an abridged and modified version of the original speeches and lives of eminent personages. The book focuses on inspiring the young minds with the speeches and lives of legendary personalities who can act as role models. The editors bring in the principle of value education whereby the students cultivate moral values from their reading. (See Appendix - I)

The language exercises at the end of selections consist of some of the following:

- Glossary
- Comprehension
- Word power: synonyms, antonyms, one-word substitutes, idiomatic expressions, Phrasal verbs
- Speech practice
- Speech writing
- Oral skills
- Oral skills – Role Play, Group Discussion
- Language development activity
- Cloze call
- Paragraph and précis writing

The main purpose of this book is to help the learner develop into an efficient user of English. Post-instruction, the inputs in the book hopefully enable the learner to use English accurately and appropriately in the day to day contexts of communication.

Inspiring Speeches and Lives is accompanied by a video CD. The CD shows four speeches delivered respectively by John F Kennedy, Martin Luther King Jr, Swami Vivekananda & Barack Hussein Obama. The CD speeches can be used in many pedagogically creative ways. The CD enables the students to gain valuable insights and imbibe vital strategies of public speaking.

5.11 LANGUAGE LABORATORY FOR I -B.TECH

In Indian traditional classroom, a language teacher finds less time to concentrate on each individual. This lacuna in the educational system can be rectified through Language laboratories. They facilitate the students to learn practical language skills according to their specific needs at their own pace. Learners can be exposed to proper accent and intonation. They can listen, repeat and practice all the language exercises with the computer and get feedback on their performance. The privacy in the laboratory is one of the most significant factors which conquers his inhibition in the process of language learning.

Language laboratory for learning Communication skills is a recent innovative method of teaching which is 'student centric' approved by the researchers, teacher and students. Computer-assisted Language Teaching is a challenging task to a language teacher who needs to know the basics of technology. Computers can never substitute teachers but they offer new opportunities for better language practice. What really matters is how the technology is used. They may make the process of language learning extensively richer, as they play a vital role in the reform of a country's educational system. The technology may be improved in the coming years to serve the next generation students' needs. Consequently, the technology may enable them to communicate effectively, carry out language

skill tasks more thoroughly and solve language learning problems more easily.

5.11.1 English Language Communication Skills Lab (ELCS)

Language laboratory is introduced in JNTU syllabus for the first year students, which gives an opportunity to become thorough in language and communication skills. English Language Communication Skills Lab (ELCS) syllabus includes Phonetics, Situational Dialogues/Role play, Oral Presentations, Extempore, Just a Minute sessions (JAM), Information Transfer, Debate, Telephone skills, and Giving Directions.

5.11.2 Advanced English Communication Skills Lab (AECS) for III/IV year B.Tech students

To equip the students with employability skills AECS Lab is introduced in III/IV year for a semester. The syllabus includes Functional English, Vocabulary Building, Group Discussion, Interview skills, Resume writing, Reading Comprehension and Technical Report Writing.

5.11.3 Methodology

The syllabus is taught through Communicative approach in the language laboratory. Most of the teachers follow activity or Task Based Language teaching. This is an instructional strategy that employs a variety of motivational techniques to make instruction more relevant. Students are engaged in activities and assigned tasks to achieve their goals. The following are the sample activities of the lab syllabus. All the activities are explained first and executed in practice later on.

5.11.4 Lab Practical Sessions

a. Role Play

A brief narrative description of the journal article, document, or resource. Role play is a dramatic technique in which individuals improvise behaviours that exemplify acts anticipated of persons involved in defined situations. The teacher instructs and motivates the students. Obviously role play scenario is self motivated because:

- Generally role play activities are fun for students, as they contain social, creative and sometimes competitive elements.
- Activities are student-centered, open-ended, and feel more like real life than lectures and tests.

Role play allows students to practice behaviors and skills, closes the gap between training and real-life, allows for immediate instructor feedback and can be used to motivate students and change attitudes. Learners demonstrate procedural knowledge in developing interpersonal communication skills. This activity is also utilized in group situations to discuss moral and ethical aspects of various issues, and to give students a sense of the duty and responsibility for a group by having students simulate their role.

Procedure

The steps to conduct a role play include, deciding on the skill and the topic, developing a scenario, assigning character roles, assigning participants and observers specific jobs, conducting a brief warm-up, running the scenario, debriefing to discuss role-play interactions and behaviors (rather than students' acting ability).

Role play activities in laboratory are conducted in the following steps:

- Situations for role play to be selected. For every role play situation, dialogues should be provided (by the teaching materials or by the teacher) or created by the students themselves.
- The students need to learn the vocabulary, sentences, and dialogues necessary for the role play situations. The instructor needs to make sure that the students know and practice the vocabulary, sentences and dialogues prior to doing the role play activities.
- Students are allowed to practice in pairs or in small groups. They exchange the roles after they have played their own roles a few times. Thus students can play different roles and practice all the lines in the role play. When they are confident enough after practice they should perform before the class.
- Practice makes the students familiar with an original role play situation. They can even modify the situations and/or dialogues to create a variation of the original role play.
- The teacher assesses the effectiveness of the role play activities and tests if students have successfully comprehended the meanings of the vocabulary, sentences and dialogues. Teacher evaluates the students in several ways.
- Students can be asked to write the words, lines, and/or dialogues in the role plays. Teachers evaluate students' understanding and comprehension observing students' interactions, practices, and performances.

Role play activities result in

Cooperation	Role-play fosters cooperation as learners work collaboratively in pairs, trios, or groups. Research has shown the advantage of group work on such aspects as promoting essential motivation; intensify self-esteem, creating caring and altruistic relationships, and lowering anxiety and prejudice.
Freedom of choice	Empowering them gives learners a sense of ownership of their learning and thereby adds to their intrinsic motivation.
Idea formation	Because learners are required to brainstorm during the dialogue construction, thinking skills are developed.

Language learning	As far as speaking is concerned, role-play enhances learners' communication skills since they are required to interact with each other, especially during the presentation stage.
Focus on realistic context	Meaningful learning leads to acquisition or long-term retention. There is meaningful learning because it is clear to the learners what they are doing in the role-play. In addition, role-play gives the learners the opportunity to utilize newly acquired topics in a realistic and communicative context.

Role Play Topics

Some of the role play topics relevant to the students are,

- Conversation between a customer and a shopkeeper.
- Conversation between two students about the selection of their courses.
- To apologize a friend for not attending his/her birthday party.
- Getting relevant information from the bank clerk.
- Discussion on sports/movies.
- Discussion on favorite subject.
- Conversation on future studies, job opportunities etc..
- Conversation between employer and employee.
- Conversation between the Chairman and the other directors of the organization.

Role play is really a worthwhile learning experience for the students. Students' speaking skills, listening skills will be improved. Role play activities bring liveliness to the class. Students learn to use language in a realistic and practical way. Therefore they can become more aware of the usefulness and practicality of English.

b. Group Discussion

Group Discussion is used as part of selection process by Organisations in their search for right candidates. Today, employees need to work in groups, not in isolation. In this aspect GD is termed to be a qualifying test. Companies conduct group discussion after the written test so as to check the interactive skills and see how good one is at communicating with other people.

The personality traits assessed through Group Discussion are:

- Communication skills
- Group dynamics
- Depth of knowledge
- Spontaneity
- Leadership qualities
- Reasoning ability
- Decision making
- Flexibility/creativity

Procedure

The teacher gives instructions on how to participate in GD. Generally the students are divided into groups consisting of 10-12 candidates. A topic is suggested, or the group can choose a topic for discussion. The topic can be of any area of science, history, culture, technology etc. They are allowed to discuss for about 15-30 minutes. The teacher will act as observer or examiner.

The candidates in the group are assessed for:

- Sound knowledge on the topic
- Communication skills
- Presentation skills
- Leadership skills
- Critical thinking, creative thinking
- Flexibility and openness
- Management skills
- Group dynamics
- Attentiveness, patience, sense of humour
- Clarity of thought
- Positive attitude
- Co-operation and co-ordination
- Team spirit
- Problem solving skills

Group Discussion Topics

Some of the topics suggested are:

- Terrorism and India
- Is there a need to protect Indian culture?
- Privatization is boon or bane
- Morals & Values among Indians are degenerating
- Effect of Television on Youth
- Should Smoking be banned completely?
- The pros and cons of having a credit card.
- Conspiracy is a very common form of political behaviour.
- Minimum Wage - Why should we have a minimum wage or why not?
- Youth entering into politics.

Group discussion as a part of the interviews takes place on the relevant and current topics.

c. Debate

Debate is an argument in which the participants have to oppose others to win by substantiating their point of view. Convincing the listener of the speaker's side of the proposition is desirable. The number of group members can be 2 to 20.

Debate Topics

Some of the topics suitable to a debate are,

- Is caste system a benefit for society
- Do you think reservations are appropriate?
- Actors entering into politics
- Development of country depends upon agriculture or computer
- We should declare war against Pakistan to fight terrorism
- Elections for student unions must be help in colleges – student must be kept away from politics
- Beauty contests must be banned in India to protect our culture
- Are TV channels misleading

- Love marriage or arranged marriage: which is better?

Procedure

Topics which have scope to debate are given to participants. The teacher gives instructions on how to participate in debate. For each group, equal time and priority is given by the examiner. Students may be provided collar mikes for performing the activity.

The participants in a debate are assessed through

- Communication skills
- Substantiating his/her point of view
- Leadership skills
- Spontaneity
- Subject knowledge
- Interpersonal skills
- Controlling the emotions

Feedback is given to the students to correct themselves. With this activity they learn how to state something, supporting a statement with valid evidence and sound reasoning, presenting ideas in a clear and effective manner to win the argument. They learn to think under pressure and make decisions quickly and accurately.

d. Interview Skills

Interview is an interaction between two or more persons usually with the question and answer pattern. The basic purpose of having an interview is to have an interaction between the prospective employee and the employer, which gives an opportunity to come out with a mutual understanding and to judge one's ability. Interview can expose the candidates' strengths, weaknesses, thinking ability and communication skills etc., It is used for the verification of data, candidate's interest and intelligence quotient.

Mock Interviews

The teacher provides an overview and speaks on social etiquette, body language and a list of expected questions of the interview. The activity on Interview skills is 'Mock interview.' The teacher acts as an interviewer in mock interview sessions.

The candidates are assessed through

- Communication skills
- Soft skills
- Technical skills
- Self confidence
- Positive attitude

Mock Interviews are like rehearsals for interview which give confidence to the students to appear for the interview immediately after completion of their B.Tech course.

Types of Interviews

i) Face to Face Interview

This type of interview includes meetings between the candidate and interviewer. It is popular with many Organizations. Here the focus should be on the person asking questions. The interviewee is to establish rapport with the interviewer and show them that his qualification and experience will benefit their organization. Following are the key skills for this type of interview

- Analytical thinking
- Communication skills
- Behavioral Skills and
- Social Skills /interpersonal skills

ii) Telephonic Interview

These interviews are increasingly used by companies as an integral part of the recruitment process. This type of interview is advantageous for the candidates who live far away and the company also gets benefitted because more number of candidates apply for the job. Majority of companies inform in advance and give the appointment to the candidates. But one should also be prepared for those who just ring. The following points are to be remembered during telephonic interview:

1. Arrange for a quite place and time to schedule the conversation.
2. Listen to the questions carefully before you answer.
3. Here voice is the key, convey energy with inflection in your voice.
4. Have a copy of resume, pen and a notepad nearby.
5. Make sure you allow enough time; interview can take upto an hour.

5.11.5 Tasks on writing skills

The formal correspondence in any organization is writing. Therefore maximum time of an employee's life is spent on writing. Engineering students need to be exposed to the following writing skills.

- Letter Writing
- Memorandum
- Resume/Curriculum Vitae
- Report
- E-mail

Procedure

The students learn the rules of writing from the teacher. The teacher gives an oral presentation over writing skills and explains practically with the help of a computer using Word document for writing styles and formats. Consequently, students are able to write the documents on the computer. The teacher facilitates the students to see on computer monitors for sample Letter writing, Memorandum, Resume/Curriculum Vitae, Report and E-mail. Then the teacher assigns tasks on writing.

The students are assessed through

- Aim of writing
- Structure
- Clarity

- Use of language
- Style/format

Writing Emails

The fast means of communication today is writing Emails. Most of the students may not understand listening to the lecture on this. Rather they may easily grasp by seeing it on a computer screen. Therefore teaching in a laboratory and with the help of computers serves the purpose. After teaching the basics the teacher can show the sample Email with guidelines and can assign the activity to be performed.

Teaching in a communicative approach way and adopting activity based learning approach in ELT breaks the monotony of a traditional ELT classroom which entirely depended on theoretical teaching where the student gets less opportunity to prove himself. The students learn freely in an interactive and independent atmosphere; realizing their own meanings, formulating their own approach to the problems and completing the task assigned. The paradigm shift of the teaching with its emphasis on the student makes the learning process more student friendly, interesting, active and practical.

The learners are benefitted by a language learning environment which suits to their life and activities. They learn actively the language which is used in practical real life situations and the introduction of authentic texts into the learning situation gives an added support to motivate them. Student's own personal experiences are important contributing elements. The classroom learning stimulates students towards the learning process. It has completely transformed the image of ELT through its innovative and practical approach that is a needs-based approach.

5.12 ASSESSMENT

The assessment and tests are conducted at regular intervals. The instruction booklet provides the schedule of the tests along with the syllabus for the tests.

5.12.1 Theory

Three Mid Term Exams are conducted as internal assessment for twenty marks (20). Each mid exam conducts descriptive (10Marks) and objective type (10 marks) tests. The syllabus for descriptive and objective tests are two Units i.e. four lessons. Two sets of question papers of descriptive type are prepared by the teacher. The objective type question paper is prepared and sent by JNTU. One and half hours time is given for writing the test. Best of three tests will be taken for 20 marks. In addition to the twenty marks, five marks are for assignments thus taking the total marks to twenty five (25).

The syllabus for I-Mid examination

Unit – I
1. Heaven's Gate from detailed text 2. Hargobind Khorana from non-detailed text

Unit – II
1. Sir. C.V. Raman from detailed text 2.Sam Pitroda from non-detailed text

End exam

The end Exam is of descriptive type for seventy five marks. The time allotted for the exam is 3 hours. Five questions have to be answered out of eight questions. Each question carries fifteen marks. The questions appear from detailed, non-detailed texts and grammar. But one finds more of text based questions and less of grammar.

5.12.2 Laboratory ELCS/AECS

The practical examinations for the English Language Laboratory practice shall be conducted as per the University norms prescribed for the core Engineering practical sessions.

For the English language sessions there shall be a continuous evaluation during the year for

25 sessional marks and 50 End Examination marks. Of the 25 marks 15 shall be awarded for day–to–day work and 10 marks to be awarded by conducting Internal Lab Test (s). The End Examination shall be conducted by the teacher concerned with the help of another member of the staff of the same department of the institution.

SECTION B

5.13 INTRODUCTION

The syllabus and the material for I- B.Tech Engineering students, Kakatiya University, was designed a decade ago. The textbook was designed to cater to the needs of the of Engineering, MBA and MCA students. Explanations and exercises on basic grammar and a few tasks based on Communicative approach form the core of the syllabus.

5.14 THE TEXT BOOKS AND THE MATERIAL

i) The book entitled *Communicative English for Engineers & Professionals,* is written by Dr. M. Surendra Kumar and Prof. G. Damodar. The book is a combination of Written Communication and Oral Communication. It covers the basics of English Grammar, Vocabulary, Written and Oral Communication skills.

ii) An Essay, "The American Scholar" by Emerson Ralph Waldo is prescribed for Reading Skills.

Extreme complexity of the essay mainly due to antique vocabulary, damages the whole interest of the students for reading. However a teacher helps overcome this hindrance. The essay is highly philosophical with verbose and involuted sentences.

5.15 LAYOUT, DESIGN AND PRICE OF THE TEXT

The size of the text book is A8 and the quality of the paper is durable. The title of the book *Communicative English for Engineers & Professionals* is striking. The font of the text is clear and the presentation of information appears to be clear. No photographs, pictures, tables, graphs and charts are used. A standard quality of editing and publishing is maintained and the price of the book is one hundred rupees. (See Appendix-I)

5.16 TIMEFRAME FOR THE PROGRAMME

English for I-B.Tech students is for an academic year. 70-80 hrs are allotted for instruction. The class work is held from October to April.

5.17 STRENGTH AND STANDARD OF THE STUDENTS

Intake for every class is 60 to 65 in Kakatiya University Engineering colleges. The students are of different standards as they come from rural and urban regions with different exposure. Overall the students of JNTU and KU have the same standard.

5.18 LANGUAGE TYPE AND CONTENT

The textbook is restricted to linguistic items. The language used for the material is within the range of Engineering graduates. (See appendix-II)

5.19 THE TEXT BOOK

Communicative English for Engineers & Professionals begins with Grammar and Vocabulary. The following guidelines and exercises on 'Sentence' are from page numbers 1 to 3. A topic from the text is taken as an example which is given under 5.21.1.

The purpose and the objectives for teaching the materials are not stated in the text book but it is mentioned in the preface that it is to help the Professionals improve their written and oral communicative abilities. No supplementary guide or instruction booklet to the teacher and the student is distributed by the university.

5.20 ORGANIZATION OF THE MATERIAL

The table of contents presents four topics giving more prominence to grammar which would be useful for the students' basic linguistic and language skills. (See appendix-II).

The textbook contains the essential linguistic items like parts of speech, tenses and structures required for an average level learner. The contents are organized under four topics. The exercises are presented with title instruction.

The four topics of the contents are:

1. Grammar and vocabulary
2. Comprehension
3. Writing skills
4. Oral communication

The following serve as the examples from the book

The Sentence

A sentence may be defined as a group of words which makes complete sense. A group of words that usually contains a subject, a verb and expresses a complete idea, statement, a question, an order or a request or an exclamation and when written in English begins with a capital letter and ends with a full stop, a question or an exclamation.

Students learning English have to learn sentence structure and their uses to improve their oral and written modes of communication. If they learn four types of sentences and their word order they will express themselves correctly and completely in any given situation or context.

There are four kinds of sentences according to word order.

1. Assertive Sentence: A sentence which expresses a statement, an assertion or a declaration.

    Structure: Subject + verb + object (s+v+o)

    Examples: $\underline{\text{Birds}}$ $\underline{\text{eat}}$ $\underline{\text{insects}}$.
             S   v   o

    $\underline{\text{Mr.}}$ $\underline{\text{Nithin}}$ $\underline{\text{writes}}$ $\underline{\text{a}}$ $\underline{\text{letter}}$.
       S   v   o

    Uses: This sentence is used to tell, to state, to declare or to assert

2. Imperative Sentence: ———————————

3. Interrogative Sentence: ——————————

4. Exclamatory Sentence: ——————————

Exercise

Write ten sentences of each kind and analyse them according to the structure.

5.21 COMPREHENSION

The following notes and exercises are from page number 135.

Comprehension refers to reading skill i.e. reading a passage critically and grasping the ideas expressed in it. It is slightly different from understanding a piece of writing.

Passages given for comprehension are intended to test the following:

1. Literal Comprehension (L) (Understanding of language)
2. Critical comprehension (C) (of evaluation)
3. Affective comprehension (A) (of reader's response)
4. Global comprehension (G) (overall understanding of a passage)

Accordingly, questions on the passage are as under:

1. Factual questions (for learning the facts)
2. Inferential questions (reading for meaning)
3. Evaluative questions (reading to decide the right things)
4. Predictive questions (reading to guess)

Comprehension is the power or faculty of understanding questions and comprehension is intended to improve or test the capacity of one's understanding of a language.

There are two types of passages generally given for comprehension.

1. Passage with four or five questions at the end to be answered in one or two sentences.
2. Passage with multiple-choice answers (particularly in competitive examinations). (Model passages with question and answers are given for practice in pages 137 to153).

5.21.1 Writing skills

The following notes and exercise are from the page numbers 154 to 158.

i) Paragraph Writing

A smallest unit of prose composition is a paragraph. It is defined as a group of sentences relating to a single topic or developing a single central idea. It is also known as thought expansion.

Generally, a proverb, a quotation, a maxim or an epigram is given for the expansion into a paragraph.

A paragraph contains a single theme or topic. All the sentences grouped should strengthen or develop the central theme explained in the first sentence. The purpose is to explain clearly without deviation or digression of theme.

The skill or ability in paragraph writing depends upon continuous practice of writing paragraphs and revising paragraphs. It requires power of comprehension and vocabulary.

Hints

1. Unity of thought and theme: —————
2. Order: —————-
3. Variety: —————

ii) Types of Paragraphs:

1. Descriptive: —————
2. Narrative: —————-
3. A paragraph of Definition: —————

An example paragraph is given on "Failures are stepping stones to success and a work sheet for students' practice from page number 156.

Worksheet:

Expand the idea contained in each of the following into a paragraph of about 100 words.

1. Slow and steady wins the race.
2. Where there is a will there is a way.
3. A bird in the hand is worth two in the bush.
4. Great talkers are never great doers.
5. Adversity is the touchstone of character.

(Notes with examples are given on Report writing and Dialogue writing also)

The students are given instructions on basic writing skills like writing correct sentences, clarity, unity of thought, cohesion, and coherence. Then they will be asked to practice writing paragraphs, letters, reports and dialogues.

The material of the text's major focus is on linguistics but it cannot cater to the needs of the learners because it has barely little material on functional English. Moreover notes on grammar is inadequate.

5.21.2 Oral Communication

The following guidelines on oral communication are in the pages 182 to 228. Notes on Pronunciation are in pages 182 to 186 which cover phonemic symbols and three term label.

Group Discussion

Notes on Group discussion are under the following heads:

- Purpose
- Organisation
- Hints for Self-improvement
- Objectives of Group Discussion

Interview Techniques

Interview tips are covered under the following:

- Self confidence
- Communication
- Dress and Personality
- Common Mistakes

The text is not comprehensive enough for today's Engineering students as their needs and demands in the market are amplified. Therefore the content and the topics on oral communication should be extensive.

5.22 THE PRESCRIBED ESSAY

"The American Scholar" is an Essay from *Selected Essays* by Emerson Ralph Waldo, prescribed for reading skills, Skimming, Scanning and note making.

The essay is scholarly and more philosophical in which an engineering student may not take interest and read it. The text is complex for the level of the student because of loquacious vocabulary which is tough to understand and irrelevant to the technical students. Extreme complexity of the lesson mainly because of vocabulary, sentence structure damage the whole interest of the students for learning (See Appendix-II).

5.23 ASSESSMENT

Three Mid Term Examinations are conducted and best of three are taken for 50 marks. The syllabus for I Mid examination is first Unit which is Grammar and vocabulary. The question paper is descriptive prepared by the teacher.

End examination is for hundred marks. One question is prescribed from the essay "The American Scholar" for 15 marks. Remaining questions are on grammar, vocabulary, Reading skills and Writing skills for 85 marks. Three hours time is allotted for writing the exam.

5.24 CONCLUSION

This chapter tried to give the critical analysis of the English syllabi of JNTU Hyderabad and KU Warangal. The Content, Material, Methodology and Assessment are looked at. Though both the syllabi use Communicative English, differences in various aspects are apparent. JNTU syllabus and the material is produced and executed methodically keeping the student's needs in view. This textbook devotes to improving student's overall social English and communication skills. The purpose of this course has always been to provide the students with a solid and broad foundation which they can apply in their social and academic situations. KU syllabus is in need of revision. A proper syllabus which will help the student in his professional and personal career needs to be devised. English in Technical Colleges is relegated to a lesser role. Students are under an illusion that they need not labour or learning English because they can get through the exams. The role of the teacher is significant. As a facilitator, the teacher has to motivate the students and point out the right direction.

C H A P T E R 6

Findings and Suggestions

6.1 INTRODUCTION

Current trends in designing English syllabus for Engineering courses focus to equip the learner with the basic linguistic knowledge and improve their communication skills. The objective of the syllabi is to train the learner with necessary communication skills. However, because of the imbalance in the level of student's knowledge coupled with aggravated syllabus, most of the students remain unsettled because of lack of communication skills. Learners either lack an interest due to the low level of the syllabus or are simply not geared to handle the language. The researchers have to admit the fact that the demands of the teaching profession have increased and it is necessary that teachers should be innovative, reflective, technology savvy and learners by nature. This chapter presents the findings of the research and makes some suggestions for the improvement of the learning atmosphere. Certain broad general factors have been identified which are equally applicable to JNTU and KU English syllabuses. The following are some of the reasons which reveal why a well-built JNTU syllabus or out-of-date KU syllabus are not able to reach the students.

6.2 ROLE OF THE TEACHER (TRADITIONAL TEACHER VS. MODERN TEACHER)

In traditional English classes the teacher followed the lecture method of teaching where the student remained passive. The needs of the students have changed which resulted in learner centered teaching where the student is more active and the teacher is a facilitator. Computer as a flexible classroom aid is used by teachers and learners in a variety of ways and for a variety of purposes. Hence the teacher in modern days should be familiar with technology in addition to the subject knowledge.

a. Implications of teaching: Traditional

The traditional teacher followed the following methodology in the class and the learner was expected to learn, memorize and repeat it passively. Traditional teaching was based more on the Behaviouristic mode of learning. The following table summarizes the teaching/ learning process.

Presentation of pattern	→	Look, listen, memorize
Elicitation of a pattern	→	Repeat with whole class
Controlled practice	→	Repeat and vary in pairs
Free practice	→	Repeat with more variation
Written reinforcement	→	Repeat in writing

b. Implications of Teaching: Revised

The teacher's role in the modern setting has undergone a drastic change. Instead of presenting, explaining, the teacher creates the situation where the student has to take note, think, discuss, find on his own and receive confirmation. The teacher tries to awaken the cognitive faculties' latent in a learner. The following table summarizes the learning/teaching process.

Look discuss and guess the point	→	Display pattern, stimulate discussion
Receive confirmation	→	Give solution on board or to groups
Repeat, vary, discuss	→	Guide, practice, encourage discussion
Invent exercises for the groups	→	Monitoring group work
Exchange questions, discuss and write answers	→	Encourage exchange, monitor writing
Discuss as a class with teacher	→	Guide discussion, summarize findings

The implication of teaching in the changed context has assigned a different role to the teacher. The teacher is not an all knowing, giver of knowledge creating awe in the students. He/She should stimulate the learner's understanding through recursive and reciprocal interactions. The teacher should not wish to become powerful, but should aim at making students more powerful. He/She is:

> More of a Facilitator
>
> Helps in self-exploration/self-reflection
>
> Evolves strategies to face challenges
>
> Allows students to unfold

6.3 ROLE OF THE STUDENT

In a learner-centered class, learners don't depend on their teacher for instructions, words of approval, correction, advice or praise. The students don't ignore each other, but they communicate among themselves freely. They are active and enthusiastic to learn. They value each other's contributions, they cooperate, learn from each other, and help each other. They do ask the teacher for help or advice if they face trouble in learning but only after they have tried to solve the problem among themselves. Learners get more benefit on working together, in pairs, in groups, and as a whole class rather than remaining as a passive listener as in a traditional class room. The teacher facilitates them to develop their language skills with the help of new teaching aids and materials.

6.4 HETEROGENEITY OF THE CLASS

Generally the text books are designed to suit a homogeneous group of learners. As the group is heterogeneous resulting in mixed ability, it leads to ineffective teaching and learning. They respond to the text variedly due to the individual differences in abilities which is challenging to a teacher to tackle with. The low level students do not show any interest in learning as they find the text too difficult for them and the bright students may feel that the text is below their stdandard. In this context the teacher is in a predicament as whether to attend low level or high level students. Streaming of students into groups according to their ability is a possible solution to the predicament of the teacher. For example, they can be grouped into average and advanced basing on self-assessment to be administered right in the beginning. The teacher can take the liberty of preparing his/her own material according to the student. The following suggestions may help in teaching these students to make teaching and learning process fruitful.

- Get the learner's profile of socio, economic, geographical and educational background.
- Estimate the standard of the student by conducting a diagnostic test.
- Classify the learners according to their standards.

- Frame the material to suit their level to bring out a better outcome.
- Evaluate the students at regular intervals for the continuous progress.
- Observe, monitor and motivate the learner constantly.
- Use various modern methods of teaching techniques to make learning process fruitful.

The teacher cannot concentrate on all the students if the strength is more than forty. But in Engineering colleges the classes are over-crowded with sixty to a hundred students. In such a scenario, the teacher plays a crucial role. It would be better if "streaming of the class" is adopted. The students can be asked to fill in a self-assessment form as soon as they start coming to classes. On the basis of the data provided they can be divided into two groups: average and advanced. The teacher is required to help the average students with additional material, exercises and other tasks. The teacher can also take the help of the advanced students by making them team leaders in the tasks or activities assigned.

6.4.1 Language levels and general traits of learners

The following table helps in identifying the various levels of students which make teaching/learning process easier and results in improving each individual student's skills. First two levels of students can be clubbed into one group and levels three & four can be combined as another level group for convenience.

Listening Level 1	Student recognizes basic words and phrases about personal and immediate concrete surroundings when people speak slowly and clearly.
Level 2	Able to understand phrases and the frequent vocabulary related to most immediate personal relevance and able to catch the main point in short, simple messages, announcements, personal information etc.
Level 3	Can understand the main points of clear standard speech on familiar matters regularly encountered at college, at bank or offices etc., and main points of radio or TV programmes on current affairs or topics of personal or professional interest when the delivery is slow and clear.
Level 4	Can understand extended speech and lectures and follow even complex lines of argument provided the topic is reasonably familiar, like TV news, current affairs programmes and films in standard dialect.
Speaking Level 1	Able to interact in a simple conversation when the speaker is ready to repeat phrases for understanding and wait for the slow reply.
Level 2	Capable to communicate in simple and routine language on tasks requiring a simple and direct exchange of information on familiar topics and activities, handle very short social exchanges even though does not clearly follow what others say.
Level 3	Able to deal with most situations likely to arise while traveling in an area where the language is spoken, can converse on topics of personal interest. (hobbies, work, travel, current events).
Level 4	Able to interact with a degree of fluency and spontaneity that makes regular interaction with native speakers quite possible. Can take active part in discussions in familiar contexts, accounting for and sustaining self views, clear descriptions on a wide range of subjects related to the field of interest, explaining viewpoint on topical issue, giving the advantages and disadvantages of various options.
Reading Level 1	Able to understand names, words and very simple sentences for example on notices and posters or in catalogues.
Level 2	Able to read very short, simple texts. Can find specific, predictable information in simple everyday material such as advertisements, prospectuses, menus, timetables, and short simple personal letters. Can connect phrases in simple way to describe experiences and events, explanations, opinions and stories.
Level 3	Can understand texts that consist mainly of high frequency everyday or job-related language, the description of events, feelings and wishes in personal letters.
Level 4	Able to read articles and reports concerned with contemporary problems in which the writers adopt particular attitudes or viewpoints and contemporary literary prose.

Writing Level 1	Able to write short, simple prose, greetings and filling in forms.
Level 2	Able to write short, simple notes and messages relating to matters of immediate need.
Level 3	Can write simple connected text on topics which are familiar or of personal interest, writing personal letters describing experiences and impressions.
Level 4	Able to write clear, detailed text on a wide range of subjects related to general interest, writing an essay, report, passing on information or giving reasons in support of or against, highlighting the personal significance of events and experiences.

6.4.2 Self-Assessment by the Student:

Diagnosis of students' language level is necessary to teach effectively to students with different levels of proficiency. Based on the basic knowledge of the language, the teacher proceeds to instruct or facilitates the students to learn according to their needs. The following ten point self-assessment form can be administered to the students immediately after their arrival to the college classes for testing their levels. This procedure enables teachers to stream them into groups:

Self-Assessment Form

a. Put a tick against the option of your choice.

1. Do you think learning English is necessary at graduation level and for engineering students?
   a. No. Not necessary.
   b. Not necessary for all because they already know the basics.
   c. Necessary for all to improve their proficiency levels of language.
2. When and where would you try to speak in English?
   Never.
   Frequently at college/with friends.
   Regularly at college/ with friends.

3. Do you read English news papers, magazines, books?
   Never.
   Some times newspaper and books rarely.
   Whenever I am free I try to read newspaper and relish reading books.
4. Do you watch or listen to English news and do you browse for English language related news?
   Never.
   Sometimes I listen to news and watch English movies.
   I make use of my leisure time by watching English news and browse for English sites.
5. Is English your medium of instruction at school?
   a. No.
   b. Yes, in the primary classes.
   c. Yes I studied in an English medium school.
6. How many words are you familiar with?
   a. 200 -500.
   b. 500 -1000.
   c. More than 1000.
7. How much can you understand while others speak in English?
   a. A word or two.
   b. Some phrases.
   c. I understand almost everything.
8. Do you speak in English or in mother tongue most of the time?
   a. I use mother tongue mostly.
   b. I try to use English only with those who cannot understand my mother tongue.
   c. I speak in English most of the time.
9. What is your proficiency level of English?
   a. I cannot get pronunciation of most of the words and fail to understand when others speak.
   b. I can understand some of the words and phrases of what others speak and I try to use the same.

    c. I can converse with others in whatever accent they speak.

10. Can you write in English?

    a. No.

    b. I can write simple sentences on general topics.

    c. I can write extensively on any topic.

b. Result of Assessment

1. Out of ten if 'c' is ticked for eight points, one has reasonable proficiency in English and has to strengthen his skills by identifying the weaknesses in various aspects of language to compete in the world.

2. If 'b' is opted more than five times, though they can carry on simple conversations in situations and use simple English, they still need to practice language fundamentals and skills.

3. Suppose 'a' is the choice for more than five points, they need meticulous practice to gain command over the basic knowledge of language and LSRW skills.

The students can be grouped into streams (at least two) of average and advanced basing on their self-assessment. The first category come under advanced and the second and third under average. The teacher needs to pay more attention to the average group by taking note of them, involving them in the class work and providing them with supplementary material. Language laboratory plays an important role here. This group should be given additional time to work with interactive software, extra tasks and activities, in order to improve their proficiency levels.

6.5 METHODOLOGY

Learner centered approach which include CALL, TBLT, CLL are now commonly adopted in the advanced English teaching classrooms. The following characteristics of LCA can be implemented by the teacher.

1. Communication in natural and meaningful contexts.

2. Integration of skills

3. Real life (authentic) materials

4. Learning by doing resulting in learner involvement

5. Class organization: individual. Pair/ group, whole

6. Focus on meaning and the use of the language

7. Extending language use beyond the class room

8. Teacher as a facilitator

9. Focus on process as opposed to product

Teaching should be through tasks, activities and interactive sessions. The organization of the class plays an important role. They have to be made to work in pairs or groups. Student-student interaction increases language use in a less threatening environment. If the whole class is involved then it has to be an interactive session. The process is emphasized rather than the product. For example, the students may be asked to recall a story they had read in the class, and narrate it to each other in pairs. Then they can become any of the characters, imagine their feelings, make up the dialogues and say it aloud before the other students. A lot of variations come up in the use of language. If the topic is letter writing, the focus should be more on what should go into the communication of a message like is it an invitation, a complaint or an application. The focus is more on the process of writing, rewriting, revising, editing etc to make the meaning more clear rather than the final product of a complete letter. A common experience is that the activities based on the text can lead from one to the other giving scope to all the skills. The teacher's role is crucial: leading, monitoring, directing and supporting the learning process.

6.5.1 Computer Assisted Language Learning

Language laboratory is a right platform for the learners because it makes teaching learning process easier and beneficial. Computer has a distinctive property which is the ability to interact with the student. Other teaching aids like teaching material, audio-visual aids can help the students in telling what is what but they cannot analyze their mistakes to correct themselves. Moreover it is an indispensable did which can be used in heterogeneous classes to cater to the needs of various levels of students. The advantages of CALL is individualization in a large class, or can work as pair or in small group on projects. It provides along with enlightenment, entertainment. Exploratory learning with large amounts of language data helps in real-life skill building. The following are the advantages of the use of computer:

- Gives individual attention to the learner and replies to him/her. It helps as a tutor assessing the learner's reply, recording it, pointing out mistakes and giving explanations.
- Directs the learner towards the correct answer.
- Offers interactive learning and can assess the learner's response.
- Generates an activity without any of the errors arising from repetition by humans.
- Can hold a very large volume of interaction and can deliver feedback to the student.
- Can accommodate different speeds of learning
- Can impose limits on the time available for answering questions (for testing purposes).

6.6 SYLLABUS REVISION

Any syllabus should not become obsolete. The same material should not be used year after year without modifications and additions. There has to be a regular evaluation by the learners and teachers, so that their difficulties and suggestions can be considered in the next revision by the textbook writers.

JNTU syllabus is revised for every three years, still there appears to be lacuna in reaching the students regarding motivation. It is agreeable that the syllabus and the material propose to advocate a communicative approach.

KU syllabus is a decade old syllabus, hence it should be revised according to the needs of the students.

6.7 TIMEFRAME

It is evident that there is no equivalence in syllabus and time allotted. JNTU fixed an academic year for I.B.Tech English in which 90 hours are given to complete the syllabus. The number of classes is still decreased by the institutions due to various reasons. It depends on the level of the student as to how much time is required to complete the syllabus. As the teachers are rated on the pass percentage, their entire time is taken up in teaching the basics for the weak students and preparing them to get through the exams. An appreciable fact however is the introduction of advanced language lab course for the outgoing students for a semester.

There is an urgent need for Planners to take note of this and allot time not only to teach basics in the first year but also life skills in the final year. Engineering students need to enhance their English communication skills and other survival skills in order to cope with the increasingly tough competition in the job market. Having only the subject knowledge in the chosen field of engineering is not going to be an assurance to get a good job or excel at the workplace. Hence it is prerequisite to introduce advanced skills laboratory as a core syllabus component.

6.8 LACK OF FACILITIES

If Computer aided teaching gives better results it also requires establishing well equipped computer language laboratory. It should have a platform of computers with latest configuration and required software. A teacher's console machine for continuous monitoring through computers, public addressing system/mike, head sets, camera for recording audio and videos of students activities, LCD Projector, television and internet connection so that the teacher produces the required teaching material. Many colleges do not have these facilities. Even if they do have, very little time is allotted to the English users for the institutions relegate the needs of English language learners to a lesser role.

A fully developed multi-media computer lab with all the required software is a must to teach and learn in the modern scenario. The managements should not ignore to provide this important facility. Often the computer lab serves the function of communications lab. The problem arising from this situation is though the students are exposed to the computer aided learning, they do not find sufficient time to practice earnestly nor can the teacher give additional assignments.

6.9 UNTRAINED TEACHERS/LACK OF TECHNICAL KNOWLEDGE IN LANGUAGE TEACHER

The technical institutes have an illusion that any person who can speak or communicate in English can teach English. They ignore the required eligibility criteria of teaching staff while recruitment. The universities can take necessary steps in this regard to monitor and train the language teachers with the necessary skills. It is the responsibility of a language teacher in modern times to update his/her knowledge in finding new techniques and methods to teach effectively.

6.10 INAPPROPRIATE ASSESSMENT

The assessment usually is on written and oral which include Internal and External exams. Mid Term Exams for theory are conducted at regular intervals. Most of the students claim that the preparation time for the exams is insufficient. It is difficult to pinpoint the reasons for the discrepancy between verbal proclamations that evaluation is crucial through all phases of instruction and the actual behavior.

The conventional evaluation system is followed to test the memory of the student rather than communicative competence of the student. As the text based questions constitute the question paper, the students tend to mug up the readymade answers which are available in the form of guides and test papers in the market. The attitude of the institutions towards the English also causes negligence in language learners. When the objective of the syllabus is to equip the learner with LSRW skills, the evaluation pattern must be to test these skills. The tests like listening to the sounds and words to test the pronunciation, listening to the sentences for proper intonation, listening comprehension, reading aloud, reading comprehension, oral presentations, dialogues, writing paragraphs, précis writing, reports, analytical essays and tests on vocabulary are appropriate to assess the learners.

Testing speaking skills is a time taking process and assessment on how to be objective becomes a fundamental question which could not be answered so far. But internal day-to-day evaluation might fetch the result. The technology can be utilized to evaluate speaking skills by taking videos with digital or handy camera which can be played again on the computer screen and can be evaluated on a set of commonly agreed parameters.

6.11 EVALUATION AND FEEDBACK

Evaluation is the last part in developing a language course. Evaluation is an essential part of learning and teaching. Evaluation applies to both students and to courses as a whole. The concepts 'evaluation' and 'assessment' are often used interchangeably. Assessment refers to the set of processes by which students learning is judged. On the other hand, evaluation is a wider term, entailing assessment, but including other processes as well. The data resulting from evaluation assist course designers in deciding whether a course needs to be modified or altered in any way that objectives may be achieved more effectively. Evaluation of the course can be done by serving questionnaire, interviewing students and teachers. But unfortunately the most important phase of the curriculum Evaluation and Feedback of the course is ignored.

SECTION A

6.12 JNTU SYLLABUS: FINDINGS AND SUGGESTIONS

6.12.1 The text and other material

The detailed and non-detailed texts have been presented excellently. The detailed text is attractive with its glossy finish, durable paper, photographs and illustrations, whereas the non-detailed text is like any other ordinary book. The selections in the book have the potential to inspire the young minds. This is the presumption of the editors given the inspirational tenor and quality of the selections. The purpose and objectives of the syllabus are given in the instruction booklet, but the text is not accompanied by supplementary material and key to the exercises. The most important skill aimed at is reading comprehension.

- It would be more helpful if paragraphs are numbered, so that it would be easier for a student when exercises are answered.

- There has to be pre-reading material introducing the author, theme and new/difficult words.

- The university prescribed the text books and relevant audio/video CDs. However, the exercises and the material in the CDs are not of considerable quantity to be incorporated in the variety of innovative teaching materials.

6.12.2 Relevance of course content

The content of text books (detailed and non-detailed) are of general interest for the student rather than specific. For instance the first lesson in Unit I is on travel. But "Heaven's Gate" is too elementary to a B.Tech level student. The exercise on word study may serve the general purpose of the learner. The vocabulary from the lesson and the exercises may be useful in general context than in academic. Of the six units except for one biographical lesson on C.V. Raman, none others deal with any science topics. The students specializing in Engineering and technology are exposed to authentic source materials in the areas of their study. Though the similarities between scientific English and general English outweigh the differences between them, still scientific English has its own register. Scientific/technical English has more of technical terms and more of complex structures. If more of lessons on science/technology were introduced there would have been scope for introducing high frequency scientific vocabulary, and frequently occurring grammar and syntactical structures. Some well-recognized examples of these are noun compounds, long pre-posed modifying clusters, reduced adjectival clauses, if clauses, passive voice etc. A few lessons on scientific topics would have been helpful for the technical student.

The lesson from second Unit is a biography of Sir C.V. Raman contains Physics terms like 'diffraction of light', 'existence of light in quanta', 'scattering of light like air molecules', 'intensity and frequency of light', 'Compton effect', 'corpuscular theory', 'feeble fluorescence' may be relevant in an academic context for engineering students. However extreme complexity of the lessons becomes a hindrance in comprehending which results in killing the interest of the learners. Another dimension to this is that the language teachers may not be proficient in imparting the technical terminology effectively. But this can be met by training the teachers whenever the curriculum changes. Hence, the teachers need to be trained to overcome this gap. The university can orient on the content prescribed.

6.13 VOCABULARY

An Engineering graduate needs to qualify English proficiency tests in order to study/work abroad. Minimum of five to ten thousand vocabulary is required to get through the competitive examinations and to communicate effectively in an academic context. But the students are apprehensive in learning vocabulary. To create interest among the students the teachers can motivate the students by adopting vocabulary skill building exercises that include the use of mnemonic techniques. Focus on semantic and situational relationships, relationships of form, word sets and collocations etc can be done through activities and games.

In addition to the text prescribed the teacher can use online teaching materials. There are many online root (prefixes and suffixes) word resources for teachers which are useful for creating both root words lesson plans and root words worksheets. Different root words can be introduced to different levels of students. An understanding of root words is particularly helpful to ESL students in terms of word recognition and phrase comprehension. Games on analogies, synonyms, antonyms, homophones, homonyms, idioms and phrases can be presented in an interesting manner with the help of language laboratory. Students can play games from basic level to advanced level at their own pace.

The teacher needs to design and use vocabulary exercises to supplement the word study material provided in the detailed /Non-detailed texts to satisfy the specific requirement of the class.

6.13.1 Fill in the blanks choosing the word from the list and complete the following sentences. (Technical extract from net)

(dawdling, synthesis, replicating, debug, versatile, fastest, restricted, demolish)

Signal generators cover a wide range of applications, from ___________ sensor signals to creating RF and the _________ high speed serial data signals. Each _________ signal generator can create a virtually unlimited number of signals - analog or digital, ideal or distorted, standard or custom. With the world's only direct____________ of high-speed serial data waveforms for simplified receiver testing, to the world's most adaptable arbitrary function generator for common stimulus signals, it has a signal generator to meet your ___________ challenge. (http://www1.tek.com/in/products/signal-generator/).

6.13.2 Write a short story using the words from the list with the help of following hints.

Word List:

Rectitude, integrity, superior, deception, loyalty, hoax, Conceit, arrogant, venture, primary, persevere, eventual

Arise, awake, and stop not - hard work – ebbs and tides in life – contribution of youth for the country – social evils and distractions – perseverance of achieving - goal in personal life and goal to bring glory to the country – every one craves for.

6.13.3 Form the words with the given prefix and suffixes and use the words in own sentences. One is done as an example.

Prefix/ suffix	Meaning	Own sentence
ambi-	Both	Very few people are ambidextrous (can use both hands), they can work fast.
bi-		
-cide		
dis-		
-ize		

6.13.4. Choose the right pair of words which has the similar correlation as the question analogy pair of words has.

1. EPIC: EPIGRAM

- A. opera: lied
- B. museum: exhibit
- C. manuscript: illumination
- D. filibuster: delay
- E. renegade: ambition

2. COMPLAIN: SNIVEL

- A. circle: wind
- B. condole: slaver
- C. grieve: sulk
- D. equip: supply
- E. inviolate: protected

6.13.5 Look at the word list and put a tick mark against the familiar words and write the meanings. Then use the words in own sentences. This can be done individually or pair or group.

6.13.6 Tick the right word for the following exercises on synonyms, antonyms, homonyms, homophones and homographs.

The exercises can be developed as follows:

1. Callow (meaning by word)
   - ○ Fragrance
   - ○ Supernatural
   - ○ Solitary
   - ○ Infantile or immature
2. Neologism
   - ○ Revival or restoration
   - ○ Not clear or uncertain
   - ○ Usage of a new word
   - ○ Strengthen
3. Acquiesce (word by meaning)
   - ○ Waive
   - ○ Miscellany
   - ○ Argot
   - ○ Remiss
4. Lower; degrade
   - ○ Abase
   - ○ Camaraderie
   - ○ Nondescript
   - ○ Disinclination

6.13.7 Select a topic on which list out as many related words as you can and share with friends. (Topics can be given by the teacher or can be chosen by the student).

6.13.8 Pick the words from the list given below, write other forms (different parts of speech) of those words and use them in different sentences.

Eg: Record
   a) I am going to submit my chemistry record tomorrow. (noun)
   b) I am recording an audio cassette now. (verb)

Address	rich	splendor	create
Brush	best	complex	determined
Guide	curious	blush	elegant
Influence	envy	distinct	inquisitive
Record	faith	enthusiastic	annoy

6.13.9 Crossword games

The following cross word game is on science vocabulary. (These games can be on general or particular topic).

Across:

2. An organism that decomposes other organisms: they have their own organisms, they have their own kingdom.
4. Something that takes up space and has mass
7. The amount of space something takes up
8. The thing you change in an experiment
9. A living thing
10. Describing words that tell how something, looks, feels tastes sounds and smells
13. The amount of matter in something
14. To get the volume of an irregular shaped object, see how much water it ————
16. Something that stays the same during an experiment
17. A big group of similar organisms

Down:

1. The measure of how tightly particles are packed in an object
3. Series of steps a scientist uses to answer a question or solve a problem
5. Scientists repeat the same experiment several times to see if the results are reliable. These repeated experiments are called ————————-
6. To get the volume of a regular shaped object, measure length, width and height and ———————— the three numbers
11. Scientists ———————- their work with one another
12. Can be trusted; if the results of several trials are the same, we can say they are ————————
15. A unit of measurement for mass.

6.13.10 Write short dialogues as pair work using idioms/phrasal verbs/one word substitutes choosing from the list.

Example dialogue:
Anoop: I just heard that Cathy got marrid.
Prem: Yea. None of us had any idea.
Anoop: I am surprised to know. Tell me the details if you know why she is in a hurry? She left us <u>in the dark.</u>
Prem: That is right. But she has to leave us anyother day if not now. Lets attend the party.
Phrase: in the dark (not knowing about something)

Word List:

Idioms/Phrases	One-word Substitutes
Sitting on the fence	Philonthropist
Tie the knot	optimist
A shot in the dark	etymology
Give away the farm	lexicographer

6.14 TEACHING MACRO SKILLS THROUGH TEXT

The syllabus integrates the four language skills. Receptive and productive are covered using strategies such as "top-down" and "bottom-up" listening and reading exercises. Both product and process oriented approaches are used to develop writing skills.

Though the main objective of the syllabus is to teach LSRW skills, it is ignored and the main focus is on teaching the text to prepare the students for writing text based question and answers. This is because,

1. some teachers are not well informed or trained to follow the objectives of the syllabus.
2. teachers are helpless to spare enough time to practice exercises on LSRW skills.
3. lack of advanced software to teach and assess every student within a short time.

The teacher has to make use of task based/activity learning to fulfill the objectives of the course. The students learn in a friendly environ rather than by listening to serious lectures. The students take active role in performing tasks. The teacher acts as the facilitator or instructor or counselor. It improves the quality of independence amongst the students encouraging them to think and communicate independently. Tasks are predominantly based on practical usage of the language that enhances the learner's ability to use their linguistic skill in real life situations and context.

Group work can be used for supporting the development of the skills, especially listening and speaking. It provides opportunities for listening to others, interaction, speculation, repetition and hearing responses. This provides an opportunity for the student's cognitive and linguistic development.

6.14.1 Reading comprehension

The entire teaching programme is geared to make the student comprehend the text. Hence teaching Reading Comprehension acquires importance for the teacher.

The students are given instructions on the text and trained to write the exams but are not trained in acquiring reading comprehension skills. The exercises in the text are not comprehensive. The teacher needs to adapt and supplement the material. The exercises on textual paragraphs should be constructed to help the learner practice the following areas, to make the teaching/learning more effective:

1. Meaning: exercises in this section give practice in the major reading comprehension skills of:
   ○ Factual recall
   ○ Finding the main idea
   ○ Understanding new vocabulary from context
   ○ Confirmation of content
   ○ Determining cause and effect
   ○ Distinguishing fact from opinion
   ○ Drawing conclusion
2. Reference: exercises in this section provide practice in identifying the antecedents of difficult references. Some sentences provide all that is needed to identify the reference. Other references have to be identified fro the surrounding material and require a more in-depth comprehension of the selection as a whole.
3. Syntax: Exercises should also focus on structures and syntactic patterns to be able to relate the structure with the text.
4. Prediction: Exercises here allow students to infer or predict what will come next in the narrative. These exercises help in saving time when skimming by preparing them to read selectively. This is done by working with thought connectors, logic, topic sentences and outline format.

A. Exercises on Reading Skills

The best way of reading is the ability to predict what will come next in a narrative. This skill will sometimes make possible to understand the idea contained in a sentence or an entire paragraph even when it contains many strange words. One can predict what comes next with the thought connectors. There are a few exercises on reading skill in the text book. To improve reading comprehension skills more exercises can be devised on text material for practice in the relevant areas.

i) Thought connectors:

Exercises which can focus on the following thought connectors can be developed:

And, besides, along (predict that information will follow)

Thus, accordingly, as a result (result or outcome will follow)

Although, but, however (contrast statement will follow)

ii) Reference

Many times learners find it difficult to decode ambiguous sentences. This can be done by identifying the antecedents of words. In this context, the reader needs to identify the context. The following line is from the lesson "Bubbling Well Road." Exercises need to be developed to make him understand such sentences. A sample is provided below:

(Choose *a* or *b* to indicate the reference for the italicized word or phrase.)

1. It was the priest who showed to me the road, but *it is no thanks* to him that I am able to tell this story.
   a. the author is thankful to the priest
   b. the author is not thankful to priest
2. *It was a thought* that caused him to break down as he stood to receive the highest accolade given to a physicist.
   a. The thought that the highest accolade is given to a physicist.
   b. Some thought which caused him to break down while receiving the highest accolade.

iii) Prediction: Logic

One's ability to predict what will follow as statement in a narrative will depend on simple logic. It is based on one's experience and is a cognitive rather than a language skill.

eg: Raman always carried simple optical tools along with him.

(Logic tells us that some reasons why Raman carries the optical tools will follow.)

(Choose *a* or *b* to predict the logic)

1. Out of this welter of subjects and books, can I pick anything really to mould my mental and spiritual outlook and determine my chosen path?
   a. I am able to pick up ideas from these books to mould my spiritual outlook.
   b. I am able to select a book from these books to mould my spiritual outlook.
2. I have generally been lucky in finding the right players for my parts, but the possibility of failure is always around the corner.
   a. I am generally lucky to find players but there are reasons which cause failure finding the players.
   b. I am generally lucky to find players but there are various reasons which cause failure in other aspects.

Exercises like the above can turn the learner into an attentive and close reader and train him in the skill of reading comprehension.

6.14.2 Recommended Reading and software

JNTU has prescribed a list of books as suggested reading for further reference. The list is exhaustive and useful for the teacher in additional material preparation. But the teacher rarely uses the additional material for want of time. An ambitious list of software is also given, most of which is not available.

SECTION B

6.15 INTRODUCTION

Kakatiya University has not revised the syllabus for a decade which points toward the fact that the syllabus is obviously outdated. The syllabus contents are helpful in improving basic linguistics rather than communication skills. The essay prescribed "The American Scholar" is not enough for improving reading skills.

6.16 THE TEXTBOOK AND OTHER MATERIAL

The text is neither accompanied by teacher's manual nor mentions the objectives of the syllabus. In fact it is not a proper text book but a book which claims to cover grammar and vocabulary, comprehension, oral communication and interview techniques. No other supplementary material is offered. The syllabus was framed when the students who entered into the stream were quiet good at English. The same syllabus is being followed for the last ten years.

The textbook is devoted to equip the learner with the basic grammar. Grammar plays a central role in the four language skills. It is generally accepted that practice can facilitate accuracy and fluency. Accuracy focuses on correct use of language which can be achieved through controlled and semi-controlled activities or practice of grammar. In fluency, after learners master rules of language, they are required to apply these in the form of spoken and written language. Ample opportunity is provided in the syllabus for practice of structures, but it lacks in the latter part of application. A close inspection of the text reveals that the treatment of linguistic items such as grammatical structures, functions, and vocabulary is disappointing. Though importance is given to oral skills, a proper relationship is not established between grammatical exercises and functional aspect of the skills. The problem with the present day students being transference of skills, KU syllabus has not addressed this problem. It is indispensable to re-structure the course and design a new syllabus for the English curriculum.

6.17 THE SYLLABUS IS NOT ABLE TO FULFILL ITS OBJECTIVE BECAUSE

No relevance of course content to the learner's need

- Heterogeneous and large classes
- Time frame
- The old methods of teaching are practiced

6.18 THE OBJECTIVES OF THE COURSE MUST BE STUDENT CENTRIC

1. To expose the students to the richness and variety of English language
2. To acquaint the students with the knowledge of phonetics and communication skills to hone the learner's language skills and interview skills and thus give career orientation to the syllabus.
3. To impart communication skills to the students by acquainting them with the structure of modern English, and to keep the students abreast of latest trends in English vocabulary.
4. To expose the students to cultural diversity and value education through the humanistic curriculum
5. To orient the students to utilize the fruits of the ICT Revolution for equipping themselves for international competitive examinations.
6. To empower the students with skills necessary for global placements.

6.19 SUGGESTIONS

The syllabus must be designed to cater to the needs of the students.

- It is necessary to introduce advanced communication skills lab in the core syllabus.
- Adequate timeframe must be set based on the syllabus content.
- Assessment must be done to test communication skills rather than testing the text based memory.
- Day to day evaluation is a more practical way of testing the students than conducting at the end of the academic year.
- Feedback on the course can be taken from the students during and after the course for a better curriculum.
- To train both the teachers and the students in the learner centric interactive methods of teaching.
- To impart soft skills, personality development and develop a sense of service-orientation.

6.20 CONCLUDING REMARKS

A textbook may be more suitable to the needs of the students but no text can appeal all the students. Apparently there is a perimeter to what teaching materials can be expected to serve in teaching and learning process. The process of language learning is far too complex to be satisfactorily catered by a deliberate set of decisions incarnated as teaching materials. It means a textbook is just a simple tool in the hands of teachers. Hence one cannot expect to work miracles with it. The text always needs to be supplemented by adequate material. What is more important than a textbook is what the teacher does with it.

C H A P T E R 7

Conclusion

Speech is a wonderful blessing but at the same time it can also be an unbearable curse. While it helps to make the intentions, desires, thoughts clear, it can also if not used correctly lead to a situation where the message is completely misunderstood. This is more so with English speaking. A right assessment of the skills necessary should be made and should be imparted to the students at this level. The purpose of this study is to look at the principles of Curriculum design, the pedagogical value and suitability of the texts, the methodology adopted in the context of students doing engineering courses.

The first chapter looks into various issues of curriculum design. Definitions of curriculum, different aspects of curriculum formulation like principles, objectives and approaches are reviewed. It provides a base for entire teaching and learning process.

The second chapter aimed to present the approaches to syllabus design which play an essential role in curriculum development. Selection of approach/approaches is considered as one of the primary tasks in a language programme. A Syllabus designer's observations on the nature of language and learning are crucial in designing the syllabus. The chapter discussed various types of approaches adopted by the course designers centered on the language teaching/learning assumptions they held.

The third chapter attempted to discuss the modern teaching methodologies Computer Assisted Language Learning, CLL and Task Based Language Teaching and how CALL and TBLT make learning process profitable. It also emphasizes the importance of macro skills in improving communication skills.

The fourth chapter presents the framework of JNTU and KU syllabi. Beginning with the text books it passes on to present the lesson titles, exercises, language laboratory syllabus with required software and finally the additional material recommended for reading. JNTU offers English twice, once in the first year and later for a semester in the III or IV year of the Engineering programme.

The fifth chapter analyses the syllabus mentioned in the IV chapter. Section A deals with JNTU syllabus. It provided with a critical evaluation of the detailed text book *Enjoying Every Day English* and Non-detailed text *Inspiring Speeches and Lives*. It analyzed critically the language laboratory syllabus of ELCS, AECS and discussed the students' assessment and tests. Section B of the Chapter deals with an evaluation of K.U. syllabus.

The sixth chapter discusses the findings of the study on various aspects of curriculum and points out the lacunae in the current syllabi. It also gives certain suggestions wherever necessary pertaining to the teaching and learning process.

It is an undeniable truth that spoken language develops as a result of exposure. While the language lab provides this exposure, conditions have to be created where the student uses the language as much as possible. Hence it is crucial to understand this process and make a conscientious effort at acquiring the sub skills which contribute to the overall speaking skill.

KU English syllabus is poorer when compared with JNTU English syllabus in various aspects. The following table illustrates the differences.

Jawaharlal Nehru Technological University, Hyderabad.	Kakatiya University, Warangal.
The syllabus is revised for every 3-5 years.	The syllabus has not been revised for ten years.
The syllabus and the material prescribed are communicative approach based: Two Text books, for Intensive and Extensive reading.	The only book prescribed is on Communication Skills which focuses on basic linguistics, and an essay for reading purpose.
The teaching material includes audio/Video CD.	No other material is provided
Language Laboratory has been introduced.	Language Laboratory is not introduced.
Internal and External (Oral, Written) practical exams are conducted for Lab syllabus.	No practical exams are conducted.
Advanced English Communication Skills Lab is introduced to III-B.Tech students.	Only for I-B.Tech
A booklet of objectives of the syllabus is supplied to the teachers and students.	No teacher's manual or objectives of the syllabus is dispensed

7.1. SUGGESTIONS AT A GLANCE:

The following are the suggestions made in the study.

1. Teacher's role is a facilitator in Learner-centered teaching. It appears that the teacher need not labour as before lecturing most of the time, but he/she has to facilitate the entire teaching/learning process. He/She has to be active, creative, a bit unconventional, subject oriented, in addition to being well versed with the modern technology.

2. Student's role is that of an active learner in today's class room. As language is not a content subject, it cannot be learnt but must be acquired. To acquire the language a lot of practice is required. A student should be active, self-motivated, interested and enthusiastic, participate in activities without inhibition and ready to work hard. He should analyse, reflect and digest what has been exposed to him. He should internalize the linguistic structures and should be able to achieve easy retrieval for communicative purposes.

3. Class composition: It is obvious that Indian class rooms are heterogeneous which a major obstacle is in the teaching and learning process. Hence it requires streaming of the students which must be done at the beginning of every teaching programme. It can be done by administering a self- assessment form to the student.

4. Methodology: The instruction should be task-based and activity-oriented as in TBLT (Task Based Language Teaching). CLL (Cooperative Language Learning) which uses pair or group work need to be the preferred mode. Rather the methodology adopted should be Learner-Centered. Employers look

for the candidates who have good communication skills, interpersonal skills and survival skills. Co-operative learning trains the learners to undertake a project as a group.

5. The JNTU Syllabus is based on Communicative Approach. Hence, the focus is on the development of the functional English of a student. The following suggestions pertain to the content and format of the text. The Selections included are of general interest. However, two or three lessons dealing with issues in general science like on environment, technology, health, human body etc, would be helpful and relevant; as these would specifically cover the type of language structures, functions, vocabulary items useful to them in their areas of study.

A second suggestion is regarding the formatting of the paragraphs in the lessons. The paragraphs in the detailed text need to be numbered. This would save time when answering reading comprehension exercises.

6. The textbook should be made mandatory in the class. It enhances the learning environment and provides an aim to the learner. To achieve this, the textbook is to be designed like a workbook so that the possession of a text becomes indispensable for the learner.

7. Objectives are broad based in JNTU Syllabus. It would be better to break them into smaller units for a clearer understanding to the teacher.

8. Teaching LSRW skills is the most important element in teaching communication skills. Mere speaking is not enough for a learner today. He/she need to be equipped with life skills/soft skills/interpersonal skills.

Teaching kinesics (Body language) is also important because communication is done not only through the words that convey the information or message, but the non-verbal behaviors too. Non-verbal communication include: facial expressions, the tone and pitch of the voice, gestures displayed through body language, physical distance between communicators (proxemics) etc. These non-verbal signals provide clues and give additional information over and above spoken (verbal) communication.

9. Exercise material provided in the book is quite useful. However a key should be provided for the exercise material. This can be given in the manual supplied to the teachers. But to accomplish the objectives more exercises need to be incorporated, or prepared by the teacher especially under reading comprehension and vocabulary category.

10. Language laboratory is to be equipped with a platform of high configured systems with internet connection and necessary furniture. To derive maximum benefits from the technology one needs to have plentiful software catering to the students of varying standards. Hence the need of the hour is to produce abundant interactive software and make it available for the colleges.

11. The examination system is more achievement oriented rather than performance oriented leading to an emphasis on grades and positions rather than issues of fluency or proficiency. Indirectly, the teacher remains in many classrooms a facilitator of examinations rather than of linguistic or communicative proficiency. Assessment of the students in engineering colleges is essentially based on testing writing with minimum

of practical and oral component. This pattern leads to memory testing only. Hence a continued assessment process which gives equal weightage to practical oral tests and writing should be considered.

12. Teachers need to update their knowledge, skills and should acquire thoroughness in their syllabus to meet the demands of globalization. Teacher training is a must for newly recruited teachers to train them in the methodology to be adopted in fulfilling the objectives of the syllabus and for incorporating technology in their teaching sessions. Orientation programmes at regular intervals for experienced teachers too is necessary to update their skills and expose them to advancements in the subject.

13. Evaluation or feedback from students and teachers is often neglected by the institutions which is the final and crucial phase of curriculum. It must be enforced seriously as it helps in devising a better syllabus for the next generation of students.

14. Timeframe is woefully inadequate for learning and practicing all the necessary components of the given syllabus. Throughout the four year programme the learner should be made to work directly or indirectly in enriching his potential. Facilities should be provided for the learner to learn at his own pace without being restrained on account of time.

Select Bibliography

I. PRIMARY SOURCES:

Emerson, Ralph Waldo. "The American Scholar 1837." *Selected Essays: Ralph Waldo Emerson*. New York: Penguin Classics, 1985. 83-106.

Rao, Rama Krishna A., ed. *Enjoying Every Day English*. Hyderabad: Sangam Books Pvt. Ltd., 2009.

Surendra Kumar, M., and G. Damodar. *Communicative English for Engineers and Professionals*. Hanamkonda: 21ˢᵗ Century Publication, 2000.

Yadava Raju, B., and C. Muralikrishna, eds. *Inspiring Speeches and Lives*. Guntur. Maruthi Publications, 2009.

II. SECONDARY SOURCES:

A. Books

Adkins, Alex, and Ian McKean. *Text to Note: Study Skills for Advanced Learners*. London: Edward Arnold, 1983.

Allen, Harold B., and Russel Campbell. *Teaching English as a Second Language*. Bombay: McGraw-Hill, 1972.

Allen, John Patrick Brierley, and Henry G. Widdowson, eds. *English in Focus*. Oxford: Oxford UP, 1974.

Allen, Virginia French. *Techniques in Teaching Vocabulary*. New York: Oxford UP, 1983.

Altman, Howard B., and C.Vaughan James. *Foreign Language Teaching: Meeting Individual Needs*. Oxford: Pergamon, 1980.

Anderson, A., and Tony Lynch. *Listening*. Oxford: Oxford UP, 1988.

Anderson, L.W., ed. *International Encyclopedia of Teaching and Teacher Education*. Oxford: Pergamon, 1995.

Appel, Joachim. *Diary of a Language Teacher*. London: Oxford Heinemann, 1995.

Arndt, Valerie, and Paul Harvey. *Alive to Language: Perspectives on Language Awareness for English Language Teachers*. Cambridge: Cambridge UP, 2000.

Arnold, Jane, ed. *Affect in Language Learning*. Cambridge: Cambridge UP, 1999.

Ashley, Joyce. *Overcoming Stage Fright in Everyday Life*. New York: Clarkson Potter, 1996.

Ashton, Patricia T., and Rodman B. Webb. *Making a Difference: Teacher's Sense of Efficacy and Student Achievement*. New York: Longman, 1986.

Bachman, Lyle F. *Fundamental Considerations in Language Teaching*. Oxford: Oxford UP, 1990.

Baker, Joanna, and Heather Westrup. *The English Language Teacher's Handbook*. London: Continuum, 2006.

Berns, Margie S. *Contexts of Competence: Social and Cultural Consideration in*

Communicative Language Teaching, New York: Plenum Press, 1990.

Bowen, Tim, and Jonathan Marks. *Inside Teaching*. Oxford: Macmillan Edn., 1994.

Brause, Rita S., and John S. Mayher, eds. *Search and Re-Search: What the Inquiring Teacher Needs to Know*. Hampshire, England: The Flamer P, 1991.

Breen, Michael p., ed. *Process Syllabuses for the Language Classroom: General English Syllabus Design*. London: Pergamon P, 1984.

Brindley, Susan, ed. *Teaching English*. London: Open UP, 1994.

Brinton, D.M.A., and M. Bingham Wesche. *Content-Based Second Language Instruction*. New York: Newbury House Publishers, 1989.

Brown, Gillian, and George Yule. *Discourse Analysis*. Cambridge: Cambridge UP, 1983.

Brown, H. Douglas. *Principles of Language Learning and Teaching*. Pearson Longman, 2007.

—. *Principles of Language Learning and Teaching*. Eaglewood Cliffs, N.J: Prentice Hall, 1980.

Brown, James Dean. *Understanding Research in Second Language Learning: A Teacher's Guide to Statistics and Research Design*. Cambridge: Cambridge UP, 1988.

—. *The Elements of Language Curriculum: A Systematic Approach to Programme Development*. Boston: Heinle & Heinle, 1995.

Brumfit, Christopher, ed. *English for International Communication*. Oxford: Pergamon, 1982.

—. *Problems and Principles in Second Language Teaching*. Oxford: Pergamon, 1980.

Brumfit, Christopher J., and Rosamond Mitchell, eds. *Research in the Language Classroom*. London: Modern English Publications in Association with the British Council, 1989.

Brumfit, Christopher J., and K. Johnson, eds. *The Communicative Approach to Language Teaching*. Oxford: Oxford UP, 1979.

Brumfit, Christopher J., and Michael Swan, eds. *Communicative Methodology in Language Teaching: The Roles of Fluency and Accuracy*. Cambridge: Cambridge UP, 1984.

Burden, Paul R., and David M. Byrd. *Methods for Effective Teaching*. Needham Heights, Massachusetts: Allya and Bacon, 1994.

Burns, Anne, and Susan Hood, eds. *Teachers' Voices: Exploring Course Design in a Changing Curriculum: National Centre for English Language Teaching and Research*. Sydney: Cambridge UP, 1995.

Burt, Marina K., Heidi C. Dulay, and Mary Bonomo Finocchiaro, eds. *Viewpoints on English as Second Language*. New York: Regents, 1977.

Byrne, Donn. *Teaching Oral English*. London: Longman, 1976.

—. *Techniques for Classroom Interaction*. London: Longman, 1987.

—. *English Teaching Perspectives*. London: Longman, New York: Macmillan, 1990.

Campbell, Donald Thomas, and Julian C. Stanley, ed. *Experimental and Quasi-Experimental Designs for Research on Teaching: Handbook of Research on Teaching*. Chicago: Rand Mc Nally College Pub. Co., 1966.

Carroll, Brendan. *Testing Communicative Performance: Principles and Practice*. Oxford: Pergamon Press, 1981.

Cazden, Courtney B. *Classroom Discourse: The Language of Teaching and Learning*. Portsmouth, NH: Heinemann, 1988.

Celce, Marianne Murica, ed. *Teaching English as a Second or Foreign Language*. London: Heinle & Heinle, 1992.

Chandler, Jon, and Mark Stone. *The Resourceful English Teacher*. New Delhi: Viva Books, 2004.

Chaudron, Craig. *Second Language Classrooms: Research on Teaching and Learning*. Cambridge: Cambridge UP, 1988.

Cole, Peter, and Jerry L. Morgan, eds. *Syntax and Semantics III: Speech Acts*. New York: Academic P, 1975.

Collie, J., and S. Slater. *Literature in the Language Classroom*. Cambridge: Cambridge UP, 2002.

Connelly, F.M., and D.J. Clandinin. *Teachers as Curriculum Planners*. New York: Teachers College P, 1988.

Cook, Vivian. *Second Language Learning and Language Teaching*. London: Hodder Education, 2008.

Coultas, Valerie. *Constructive Talk in Challenging Classrooms: Strategies for Behaviour Management and Talk-Based Tasks*. London: Routledge, 2007.

Crombie, Winifred. *Discourse and Language Learning: A Relational Approach to Syllabus Design*. Oxford: Oxford UP, 1985.

Crystal, David. *The Cambridge Encyclopedia of the English Language*. Cambridge: Cambridge UP, 1995.

—-. *English as a Global Language*. Cambridge: Cambridge UP, 1997.

Cunningsworth, Alan. *Choosing Your Coursebook*. Oxford: Heinemann, 1995.

Cunningsworth, Alan, and Brian Tomlinson. *Evaluating and Selecting EFL Teaching Materials*. London: Heinemann, 1984.

Currie, William Brown. *New Directions in Teaching English Language*. London: Longman, 1973.

Davies, Alan. *Principles of Language Testing*. Oxford: Basil Blackwell, 1990.

Dubin, Fraida, and Elite Olshtain. *Course Design: Developing Programs and Materials for Language Learning*. New York: Cambridge UP, 1986.

Davies, Keith. *Human Behavior at Work*. Virginia: Diane Publishing Co., 1994.

Dudley-Evans, Tony, and Maggie Jo St.John. *Developments in English for Specific Purposes: A Multi-Disciplinary Approach*. Cambridge: Cambridge UP, 1998.

Duff, Tony, ed. *Explorations in Teacher Training: Problems and Issues*. Harlow: Longman, 1988.

Eisner, Elliot W., and Elizabeth Vallance. *Conflicting Conceptions of Curriculum*. Berkeley, CA: McCutchan, 1974.

Ellis, Rod. *Task-based Language Learning and Teaching*. New York: Oxford UP, 2003.

—-. *Understanding Second Language Acquisition*. Oxford: Oxford UP, 1985.

Feez, Susan. *Text-Based Syllabus Design*. Sydney: National Center for English Teaching and Research (NCETR), 1998.

Finocchiaro, M., and C.J. Brumfit. *The Functional-Notional Approach: From Theory to Practice*. New York: Oxford UP, 1983.

Firth, Alan. *The Discourse of Negotiation: Studies of Language in the Work Place*. Oxford: Pergamon, 1995.

Flower, Dew J., and L. Miller. *Second Language Listening: Theory and Practice*. Cambridge: Cambridge UP, 1996.

Freeman, Donald. *Techniques and Principles in Language Teaching*. Oxford: Oxford UP, 2000.

Freeman, Donald, and Jack C. Richards, eds. *Teacher Learning in Language Teaching*. New York: Cambridge UP, 1996.

Freeman, Richard, and Roger Lewis. *Planning and Implementing Assessment*. London: Routledge, 2005.

Gautam, Kripa K. *English Language Teaching: A Critical Study of Methods and Approaches*. New Delhi: Harman Publishing House, 1988.

Graves, Kathleen. *Teachers as Course Developers*. Cambridge: Cambridge UP, 1996.

—-. *Designing Language Courses: A Guide for Teachers*. Boston: Heinle & Heinle, 2000.

Hadfield, Jill. *Advanced Communication Games*. Edinburgh: Thomas Nelson & Sons Ltd., 1987.

—-. *Classroom Dynamics*. Oxford: Oxford UP. 1992.

Haines, S. *Projects for the EFL Classroom*. London: Nelson, 1989.

Halliday, Michael Alexander Kirkwood. *Explorations in the Functions of Language*. London: Edward Arnold, 1975.

—. *Language as Social Semiotic*. London: Edward Arnold, 1978.

—. *Explorations in the Functions of Language*. London: Edward Arnold, 1973.

Hari Prasad, M., et al. *Strengthen Your Steps: A Multimodal Course in Communication Skills*. Guntur (India): Maruthi Publications, 2011.

Harmer, Jeremy. *How to Teach English*. New Delhi: Dorling Kindersley, 2006.

—. ed. *The Practice of English Language Teaching*. England: Pearson Longman, 1996.

Harrison, Brian. *English as a Second and Foreign Language*. London: Edward Arnold, 1973.

Howatt, Anthony Philip Reid. *A History of English Language Teaching*. Oxford: Oxford UP, 1984.

Hutchinson, Tom, and Alan Waters. *English for Specific Purposes: A Learning-centered Approach*. London: Cambridge UP, 1987.

Johnson, Keith. *Communicative Syllabus Design and Methodology*. London: Pergamon Press, 1982.

Johnson, Keith, and Keith Morrow. *Communication in the Classroom*. London: Longman, 1981.

Jordan, R.R. *English for Academic Purposes*. Cambridge: Cambridge UP, 1997.

Kelly, A.Vic. *The Curriculum: Theory and Practice*. London: Harper and Row, 1977.

King, P. *Teaching English: A Teaching Skills Workbook*. Hong Kong: Macmillan Edn., 1985.

Knowles, Malcolm S. *The Modern Practice of Adult Education*. New York: Association Press, 1970.

Kudchedkar, Shirin, ed. *Readings in English Language Teaching in India*. Hyderabad: Orient Longman, 2002.

Lesikar V. Raymond, and Marie E. Flately. *Basic Business Communication: Skills for Empowering the Internet Generation*. New Delhi: Tata McGraw Hill Publishing Co. Ltd., 2002.

Leithwood, Kenneth A., ed. *Studies in Curriculum Decision Making*. Toronto: OISE P, 1982.

Littlewood, William. *Communicative Language Teaching*. Cambridge: Cambridge UP, 1981.

Lynch, Brain K. *Language Programme Evaluation: Theory and Practice*. Cambridge: Cambridge UP, 1996.

Lynch, Tony. *Study Listening*. Cambridge: Cambridge UP, 1983.

Maley, A., and S. Moulding. *Learning to Listen*. Cambridge: Cambridge UP, 1981.

Martinez Pons, M. *The Continuum Guide to Successful Teaching in Higher Education*. London: Viva-Continuum, 2006.

McDonough, Jo, and Christopher Shaw. *Materials and Methods in ELT*. Oxford: Blackwell, 1993.

McLaughlin, Barry. *Theories of Second Language Learning*. London: Edward Arnold, 1987.

Meenakshi, M.A. *Modern Trends in Educational Evaluation and Measurement*. Chandigarh: Arun Publishing House, 1994.

Moore, John. *Reading and Thinking in English: Discourse in Action*. Oxford: Oxford UP, 1980.

Morrow, Keith. *Skills for Reading*. Oxford: Oxford UP, 1980.

Munby, John. *Communicative Syllabus Design*. Cambridge: Cambridge UP, 1978.

Murphy, John., and Patricia Byrd, eds. *Understanding the Course We Teach: Local Perspectives on English Language Teaching*. Ann Arbor: Uni. of Michigan P, 2001.

Nirupama, K., et al. *Step by Step: Learning Language and Life Skills*. New Delhi (India): Pearson, 2012.

Nunan, David. *The Learner-centered Curriculum*. Cambridge: Cambridge UP, 1988.

—. *Designing Tasks for the Communicative Classroom*. Cambridge: Cambridge UP, 1989.

—. *Language Teaching Methodology. A Textbook for Teachers*. London: Prentice Hall International, 1991.

—-. *Research Methods in Language Learning.* Cambridge: Cambridge UP, 1992.

—-. *Second Language Teaching & Learning.* Boston: Heinle and Heinle, 1999.

O'Donnell, William Robert, and Loreto Todd. *Variety in Contemporary English.* London: Routledge, 1995.

Oliver, I. Albert. *Curriculum Improvement: A Guide to Problems, Principles and Processes.* New York: Harper and Row, 1977.

Olsen, R., and Spencer Kagan. *Cooperative Learning: A Teacher's Resource Book.* Eaglewood Cliffs, NJ: Prentice Hall, 1992.

Omaggio, Alice Hadley. *Teaching Language in Context: Proficiency -Oriented Instruction.* Boston: Heinle & Heinle, 1986.

Oxford, Rebecca L. *Language Learning Strategies: What Every Teacher Should Know.* Rowley, Mass: Newbury House, 1990.

Palmer, Harold Edward. *The Principles of Language Study.* Reprinted Oxford: Oxford UP, 1964.

Peck, Antony. *Language Teachers at Work: A Description of Methods.* London: Prentice Hall, 1988.

Prabhu, N. S. *Second Language Pedagogy.* Oxford: Oxford UP. 1987.

Rea-Dickins, P., and E.Germaine. *Evaluation.* Oxford: Oxford UP, 1992.

Richards, Jack C., and Theodore Rodgers. *Approaches and Methods in Language Teaching.* Cambridge: Cambridge UP, 2001.

Richards, Jack C. *Curriculum Development in Language Teaching.* Cambridge: Cambridge UP, 2001.

Richterich, Rene. *Introduction to Case Studies in Identifying Language Needs.* Oxford: Pergamon, 1983.

Rivers, Wilga M. *Teaching Foreign Language Skills.* Chicago: Chicago UP, 1981.

Ruggiero, Vincent Ryan. *Teaching Thinking Across the Curriculum.* New York: Harper and Row, 1988.

Sauvignon, S. *Communicative Competence: Theory and Classroom Practice.* MA: Addison-Wesley, 1983.

Seelye, H. Ned. *Teaching Culture: Strategies for Inter-cultural Communication.* Lincolnwood, IL: National Textbook Company, 1984.

Simpson, Paul. *Language through Literature: An Introduction.* London: Routledge, 1997.

Scarbrough, David. *Reasons for Listening.* Cambridge: Cambridge UP, 1984.

Skehan, Peter. *Individual Differences in Second Language Learning.* London: Edward Arnold, 1989.

Stenhouse, Lawrence. *An Introduction to Curriculum Research and Development.* London: Heinemann, 1975.

Stern, Hans Heinrich. *Fundamental Concepts of Language Teaching.* Oxford: Oxford UP, 1983.

—-. *Issues and Options in Language Teaching.* London: Oxford UP, 1992.

Stevens, Peter. *Teaching English as an International Language.* Oxford: Pergamon, 1980.

Taba, Hild. *Curriculum Development: Theory and Practice.* New York: Brace & World, 1962.

Thornbury, Scott. *How to Teach Vocabulary.* Essex: Pearson Edn. Ltd., 2002.

Tomlinson, Brian, ed. *Materials Development in Language Teaching.* Cambridge: Cambridge UP, 1988.

Tudor, Ian. *Learner-centeredness as Language Education.* Cambridge: Cambridge UP, 1996.

Tyler, Ralph W. *Basic Principles of Curriculum and Instruction.* Chicago: Chicago UP, 1949.

Ur, Penny. *A Course in Language Teaching.* Cambridge: Cambridge UP, 2005.

Van Lier, Leo. *Interaction in the Language Curriculum: Awareness, Autonomy and Authenticity.* London: Longman, 1996.

Wallace, Michael J. *Training Foreign Language Teachers: A Reflective Approach.* Cambridge. Cambridge. UP, 1991.

West, Michael. *Learning to Read a Foreign Language*. London: Longman, Green and Co., 1926. 1963.

—-. *A General Service List of English Words*. London: Longman, Green and Co., 1953.

White, Ronald V. *The ELT Curriculum*. Basil Blackwell, Oxford: Oxford UP, 1988.

Widdowson, Henry G. *Teaching Language as Communication*. Oxford: Oxford UP, 1978.

—-. *Stylistics and the Teaching of Literature*. Oxford: Oxford UP, 1979.

—-. *Learning Purpose and Language Use*. Oxford: Oxford UP, 1983.

Wilkins, D.A. *Notional Syllabuses*. Oxford: Oxford UP, 1976.

Willis, Dave. *The Lexical Syllabus: A New Approach to Language Teaching*. London: Oxford UP, 1989.

Wilson, Geoffrey H. *Curriculum Development and Syllabus Design*. Oxford: Oxford UP, 1976.

Yalden, Janice. *The Communicative Syllabus: Evaluation, Design and Implementation*. Oxford: Pergamon, 1983.

Yardi, V.V. *Teaching English in India Today*. Aurangabad: Parimal, 1977.

B. Articles

Allwright, D. "Turns, Topics and Tasks: Patterns of Participation in Language Learning and Teaching." *Discourse Analysis in Second Language Research*. Ed. Larsen Freeman. Rowley M A: Newbury House, 1980. 165-187.

Alptekin, Cem, and Margaret Alptekin. "The Question of Culture: EFL Teaching in Non-English speaking Countries." *ELT Journal* 38.1 (1984): 14-20.

Ames, C., and J. Archer. "Achievement Goals in the Classroom: Students' Learning Strategies and Motivation Process." *Journal of Educational Psychology* 80 (1988): 260-267.

Anderson, Neil, et al. "An Exploratory Study in to the Construct Validity of a Reading Comprehension Test: Triangulation of Data Sources." *Language Testing* 8.1 (1991): 41-66.

Anton, Marta M. "Using Ethnographic Techniques in Classroom Observation: A Study of Success in a Foreign Language Class." *Foreign Language Annals* 29.4 (1996): 551-561.

Antonek, Janis L., et al. "The Student Teacher Portfolio as Autobiography: Developing a Professional Identity." *The Modern Language Journal* 81.1 (1997): 15-27.

Arndt, Valerie. "Six Writers in Search of Texts: A Protocol-Based Study of L1 and L2 Writing." *ELT Journal* 41.4 (1987): 257-267.

Barnett, Jenny. "Notional/Functional Approaches." *Annual Review of Applied Linguistics. Ed.* Robert Kaplan, L. Randall, Jones and G. Richard Tucker Rowley, Mass: Newbury House, 1980. 43-57.

Belcher, Diane D. "English for Specific Purposes: Teaching to Perceived Needs and Imagined Futures in Worlds of Work, Study and Everyday Life." *TESOL Journal* 40 (2006):133-156.

Benesch, Sarah. "Needs Analysis and Curriculum Development in EAP: An Example of Critical Approach." *TESOL Journal* 30 (1996): 723-738.

Ben, Perez M. "The Concept of Curriculum Potential: Curriculum Theorizing." *Journal of Thought* 5 (1975): 151-159.

Benson, Malcolm J. "Attitudes and Motivation towards English: A Survey of Japanese Freshmen." *RELC Journal* 22.1 (1991): 34-48.

Berwick, Robert. "Needs Assessment in Language Programming: From Theory to Practice." *The Second Language Curriculum*. Ed. R.K. Johnson New York: Cambridge UP, 1989. 51-60.

Blue, George, and Peter Grundy. "Team Evaluation of Language Teaching and Language Courses." *ELT Journal* 50.3 (1996): 244-250.

Breen, Michael P., and Christopher N. Candlin. "The Essentials of a Communicative Curriculum in Language Teaching." *Innovation in English Language Teaching: A Reader.* Ed. D. R. Hall and A. Hewings. London: Routledge, 2001. 9-26.

Brennan, Moya, and Margaret Van Naerssen. "Language and Content in ESP." *ELT Journal* 43.3 (1989): 196-205.

Brown, C. A., and Cooney, T. J. "Research on Teacher Education A Philosophical Orientation." *Journal of Research and Development in Education* 15.4 (1982): 13-18.

Bruce, I. "Syllabus Design for EAP Writing Courses: A Cognitive Approach." *Journal of EAP* 4 (2005): 239-256.

Brumfit, Christopher J. "A Review of Wilkins Notional Syllabuses." *ELT Journal* 33.1 (1978): 14-18.

Burnaby, Barbara, and Yilin Sun. "Chinese Teachers' Views of Western Language Teaching:Context Informs Paradigms." *TESOL Quarterly* 23.2 (1989): 219-238.

Canale, Michael. "On Some Dimensions of Language Proficiency." *Issues in Language Testing Research.* Ed. J.W. Oller. Rowley M.A: Newbury House Publishers, Inc. (1983): 333-342. Print.

—-. "Communicative Competence to Communicative Language Pedagogy." *Language and Communication.* Ed. J.C. Richards and R.W. Schmidt. London: Longmon 1983. 2-27. Print.

Canale, Michael, and Merril Swain. "Theoretical Bases of Communicative Approaches to Second Language Teaching and Testing." *Applied Linguistics. Oxford Journal* 1.1 (1980): 1-47.

Carroll, John Bissel. "Implications of Aptitude Test Research and Psycholinguistic Theory for Foreign Language Teaching." *International Journal of Psycholinguistics* 11.2 (1973): 5-13.

Carroll, John B. "Conscious and Automatic Processes in Language Learning." *Canadian Modern Language Review* 37.3 (1981): 462-474.

Chambers, Fred. "Seeking Consensus in Coursebook Evaluation." *ELT Journal* 51(1997): 29-35.

Cook, Vivian James. "Bridging the Gap between Computing and Language Teaching." *ELT Documents* 122.13 (1985): 21-24.

Corder, S. Pit. "Review of Stephen Krashen's Second Language Acquisition and Second Language Learning and Principles and Practice in Second Language Acquisition." *International Review of Applied Linguistics* 5.1 (1984): 161-170.

Davies, Alun. "What do Learners Really Want from their EFL Course?" *ELT Journal* 60.1 (2006): 3-12.

Ellis, Greg. "How Culturally Appropriate is the Communicative Approach?" *ELT Journal* 50.3 (1996): 213-218.

Ellis, Rod. "Informal and Formal Approaches to Communicative Language Teaching." *ELT Journal* 36. 2 (1982): 73-82.

—-. "The empirical evaluation of language teaching materials." *ELT Journal* 51.1 (1997): 36-41.

Grabe, W. "Current Developments in Second Language Reading Research." *TESOL Quarterly* 25.3 (1991): 375-406.

Grey, John. "The ELT Coursebook as Cultural Artifact." *ELT Journal* 54.3 (2000): 274-283.

Hawkey, R. "Needs Analysis and Syllabus Design for Specific Purposes." *Foreign Language Teaching Meeting Individual Needs.* Ed. H.B.Actman and C.V. James. London: Pergamon, 1980: 81-93.

Hiep, Pham Hoa. "Communicative Language Teaching, Unity within Diversity." *ELT Journal* 61.3 (2007): 193-201.

Horwitz, Elaine K., Michael B. Horwitz, and Joann Cope. "Foreign Language Classroom

Anxiety." *Modern Language Journal* 70.2 (1986):125-132.

Huckin, Thomas, and J. Bloch. "Strategies for Inferring Word-meanings in Context: A Cognitive Model." *Second Language, Reading and Vocabulary Acquisition*. Ed. T. Huckin. Ablex, NJ: Norwood, 1993. 153-180.

Hutchinson, Tom, and Alan Waters. "How Communicative is ESP?" *ELT Journal* 38. 2 (1984): 108-113.

Hutchinson, Tom, and Eunice Torres. "The Textbook as Agent of Change." *ELT Journal* 48.4 (1994): 315-328.

Savignon, Sandra J. "Communicative Language Teaching." *Theory into Practice* 26.4 (1987): 235-242.

Johnson, Keith. "The Production of Functional Materials and their Integration with Existing Language Teaching Programmes." *ELT Documents* 76.1 (1976): 16-25.

Krashen, Stephen D. "The Monitor Model for Adult Second Language Performance." *Viewpoints on English as a Second Language*. Ed. M. Burt, H. Dulay and M. Finocchiaro. New York: Regents, 1977. 151-156.

Lawler, John, and Larry Selinker. "On Paradoxes, Rules and Research in Second Language Learning." *TESOL Quarterly* 21.1 (1971): 27-43.

Markee, Numa. "Towards an Appropriate Technology Model of Communicative Course Design." *English for Specific Purpose* 5.2 (1986): 161 -72.

McGroarty, Mary. "The Benefits of Cooperative Learning Arrangements in Second Language Instruction." *NABE Journal* 13.2 (1989): 127-143.

Nunan, D. "Communicative Language Teaching: Making it Work." *ELT Journal* 41.2 (1988): 136-45.

O'Neill, Robert. "Why Use Textbooks?" *ELT Journal* 36.2 (1982): 104-111.

Sheldon, Leslie E. "Evaluating ELT textbooks and materials" *ELT Journal* 42.4 (1988): 237-246.

Siemani, Ashley. "Evaluation of Classroom Interaction." *Evaluating Second Language Education*. Ed. J.C. Alderson and A. Beretta. Cambridge: Cambridge UP, 1992. 197-221.

Stern, Hans Heinrich. "Introduction, Review and Discussion." *General English Syllabus Design*. Ed. C J. Brumfit. Oxford: Pergamon, 1984. 110-118.

Tickoo, M. L. "Book Review: English for Specific Purpose: A Learning-centered Approach." *RELC Journal* 2 (1987): 92-99.

White, Cynthia J. "Negotiating Communicative Language Learning in a Traditional Setting." *ELT Journal* 43.3 (1989): 213-220.

Williams, David. "Developing Criteria for Textbook Evaluation." *ELT Journal*. 37.3 (1983): 251-255.

C. Webliography

Andreea, Cervatiuc. "ESL Vocabulary Acquisition: Target and Approach." *TESOL Journal* 14.1 (2008): n. pag. Web. 20 June 2009. <http://iteslj.org/Articles/Cervatiuc-VocabularyAcquisition.html>.

Basturkmen, H. "Refining Procedures: A Needs Analysis Project, at Kuwait University." *English Teaching Forum* 36.4 (1998):1-7. Web. 12 March 2008. <http://exchanges.state.gov/forum/vols/vol36/no4/p2.htm>.

Dave, Willis. "The Language Syllabus: Building Language Study into a Task-based Approach." *IH Journal* 30.23 (2011): n. pag. Web. 2 December 2011. <http://ihjournal.com/the-language-syllabus-building-language-study-into-a-task-based-approach-by-dave-willis-2>.

Eddie, White. "Assessing the Assessment: An Evaluation of a Self assessment of a Class Participation Procedure." The Asian Quarterly Journal 11.3 (2009): n. pag. Web. 11 October 2010. <http://asian-efl-journal.com/quarterly-journal/2009/09/25/assessing-the-assessment-

an-evaluation-of-a-self-assessment-of-a-class-participation-procedure/>.

Fadi Maher, Al-Khasawneh. "Vocabulary Learning Strategies: A Case of Jordan University of Science and Technology." Web. 14 June 2010.
<http://esp-world.info/Articles 34/Al Khasawneh Abstract.htm>.

Gnutzmann, Claus, and Intemann Frauke, eds. "The Globalization of English and the English Language Classroom." *ELT Journal* 60.2 (2006):204-205. Web. 12 June 2008.
<http://eltj.oxfordjournals.org/content/60/2/204.short>.

James, Hunter. "Small Talk: Developing fluency, accuracy and complexity in speaking." *ELT Journal* 66.1 (2012): 30-41. Web. 15 January 2012.
< http://eltj.oxfordjournals.org/content/66/1.toc>.

James Venema. "Discussions in the EFL Classroom: Some Problems and How to Solve Them." *TESOL Journal* (2006): n. pag. Web. 10 August 2009.
<http://iteslj.org/Techniques/Venema-EFLDiscussions.html>.

Jon, Shave. "A Teacher Friendly Process for Evaluating and Selecting ESL/EFL Course books." *TESOL Journal* XVI.11 (2010): n. pag. Web. 18 May 2011.
< http://iteslj.org/Articles/Shave-CourseBookEval-uation.html>.

Joseph, C. Mukalel. "Approaches to English Language Teaching." Web. 10 March 2009.
<http://books.google.co.in/books/about/Ap-proaches To English LanguageTeach-ing.?id=RGkBhcwqlWMC&redir esc=y>.

Ken, Hyland. "English for Specific Purposes: Some Influences and Impacts." Web. 22 April 2009.

<http://www.springerlink.com/content/p3320731v07x48t7/>.

Kenneth, Beare. "Improve Reading Skills." 23 May 2011. Web.
<http://esl.about.com/od/englishreadingskills/a/readingskills.htm>.

Kristen, Gatehouse. "Key Issues in English for Specific Purposes (ESP) Curriculum Development." *The Internet TESOL Journal* 8.3 (2009): n. pag. Web. 20 August 2007.
<http://iteslj.org/Articles/Gatehouse-ESP.html>.

Lee, William R. "Notional Syllabuses, Construction for Foreign-Language Teaching: Reconciling the Approaches." *ELT Documents* 1980. 81-85. Web. 12 May 2009.
<http://fel.uqroo.mx/adminfile/files/memorias/Articulos Mem FONAEL III/Nunez y Bodegas Irma Dolores.pdf>.

Rebecca, Belchamber. "The Advantages of Communicative Language Teaching." *TESOL Journal* 13.2 (2007): Web. 12 May 2011.
<http://iteslj.org/Articles/Belchamber-CLT.html>.

Roger, Hunt. "Task-based Language Learning and Teaching." Web. 25 March 2011.
<http://www.ihes.com/bcn/tt/articles/tbl.html>.

Venkatraman G., and Prema P. "English Language Skills for Engineering Students: A Needs Survey." *ESP World* 16 (2007): n. pag. Web.11 June 2010.
<http://www.esp-world.info/articles 16/Skills.htm>.

Yiching, Chen. "Barriers to Acquiring Listening Strategies for EFL Learners and their Pedagogical Implications." *TESOL Journal* 8.4 (2005): n. pag. Web. 2 January 2011.
<http://www.cc.kyoto-su.ac.jp/information/tesl-ej/ej32/a2.html>